ENGLISH LITERATURE
FROM THE **OLD ENGLISH PERIOD** THROUGH THE **RENAISSANCE**

THE BRITANNICA GUIDE TO WORLD LITERATURE

ENGLISH
LITERATURE
FROM THE OLD ENGLISH PERIOD
THROUGH THE RENAISSANCE

EDITED BY J.E. LUEBERING, MANAGER AND
SENIOR EDITOR, LITERATURE

IN ASSOCIATION WITH

ROSEN
EDUCATIONAL SERVICES

Published in 2011 by Britannica Educational Publishing
(a trademark of Encyclopædia Britannica, Inc.)
in association with Rosen Educational Services, LLC
29 East 21st Street, New York, NY 10010.

Distributed exclusively by Rosen Educational Services.
For a listing of additional Britannica Educational Publishing titles, call toll free (800) 237-9932.

First Edition

Britannica Educational Publishing
Michael I. Levy: Executive Editor
J.E. Luebering: Senior Manager
Marilyn L. Barton: Senior Coordinator, Production Control
Steven Bosco: Director, Editorial Technologies
Lisa S. Braucher: Senior Producer and Data Editor
Yvette Charboneau: Senior Copy Editor
Kathy Nakamura: Manager, Media Acquisition
J.E. Luebering: Senior Editor, Literature

Rosen Educational Services
Jeanne Nagle: Senior Editor
Joanne Randolph: Editor
Nelson Sá: Art Director
Cindy Reiman: Photography Manager
Matthew Cauli: Designer, Cover Design
Introduction by Rebecca Carranza

Library of Congress Cataloging-in-Publication Data

English literature from the Old English period through the Renaissance / edited by J.E.
Luebering.—1st ed.
     p. cm.—(The Britannica guide to world literature)
Includes bibliographical references and index.
ISBN 978-1-61530-110-2 (library binding)
    1. English literature—History and criticism. 2. English literature—Old English, ca. 450–1100—
History and criticism. 3. English literature—Middle English, 1100–1500—History and criticism.
4. English literature—Early modern, 1500–1700—History and criticism. I. Luebering, J. E.
PR83.E62 2010
820.9—dc22

                                                                    2009047904

Manufactured in the United States of America

On the cover: William Shakespeare *(foreground)* and Geoffrey Chaucer are two of the most
recognizable and important luminaries of early English literature. *Oli Scarff/Getty Images
(Shakespeare); Hulton Archive/Getty Images (Chaucer)*

On page 10: A stained glass window depicting printer William Caxton as he presents his first
printed page to King Edward IV and his queen. *Ernest Heimann/Hulton Archive/Getty Images*

CONTENTS

10

30

43

57

65

87

89

99

118

136

166

London Theatres *c.*

179

INTRODUCTION

Perhaps the best way to start appreciating early English literature is to not think of it as literature at all. The earliest stories in the English language were not written for academic study but as an extension of the oral tradition of relating grand and fanciful tales for entertainment. These stories, then, were the blockbuster summer movies of their day--tales of adventure and romance, with brave knights, beautiful women, horrible monsters, and mysterious spirits.

Over the centuries these stories became a part of English literature, and along the way, the gripping manner in which they were told made the leap from word of mouth to the page. This book will show how that transition was made as it takes you on a journey through time and literary development.

To study English literature from the Old English period to the Renaissance is to witness the movement from one-dimensional action stories and religious lessons to stories with more subtleties of plot and character development and the development of language usage from simple conventions to new uses of sound and meaning. In short, this period began the rich tradition of English literature that continues to grow today.

Tracing when exactly this evolution started involves an element of mystery. Because there was no formal publishing as we know it today, the exact dates when many important works of early English literature were written are not known. Some dates can be estimated based on what is known about the life span of the author, while others can be placed in history according to their references to significant events. In general, the Old English period is considered to extend from the 7th to the 11th centuries.

These dates are significant because of the tumultuous history of England during this time. Various waves of invaders brought different languages and cultural traditions to the island, so the original language of the inhabitants was enriched by Germanic and Norman influences, as well as by the Latin used extensively by members of the clergy.

It was breaking away from Latin--then considered the language of choice for educated writing--that first distinguished literary development in England from that of the rest of Europe. A cowherd from northern England named Caedmon began composing verses inspired by Christian scripture in his native language, and though only one of these, the "Hymn of Creation," survives, the composition of verse in the vernacular became popular in England.

The style of poetry that emerged from these early verses relied on fairly narrow conventions usually based around a four-stress metre with an alliterative link between the two halves of each line. Standard images and descriptions were used—again, the emphasis at first was not on originality of language, but on getting the story across. These stylistic conventions for Old English poetry remained virtually unchanged for 400 years. Most of the verse that survives from this period is known through four manuscripts from around the year 1000—the Beowulf Manuscript, the Exeter Book, the Junius Manuscript, and the Vercelli Book.

It should be noted that besides being ahead of vernacular European poetry of the time, English verse was also more advanced than English prose during most of the Old English period. Most prose works in English at this time consisted either of translations of Scripture or practical tracts dealing with law or medicine.

The Norman invasion in 1066 signaled the beginning of the end for the Old English period. Anglo-Norman (a French dialect) provided a rival to the English language, though the Norman influence ultimately contributed significantly to English. This transitional period is referred to as the Middle English period.

English prose works from the early stages of this period are relatively few, in part because writers were split among those using English, those using Anglo-Norman, and those using Latin. One fortunate by-product of the linguistic split is that some earlier works were translated into the newer, Norman-influenced language in the early 13th century, and as a result these survive to this day.

Even as the language evolved, prose works continued to mainly be of a religious nature, including several works by a mystic hermit named Richard Rolle in the 14th century, an earlier group of works known as the Katherine Group from the 13th century, and a guidebook for women recluses called the *Ancrene Wisse*. This last work marks a significant step forward in sophistication of writing style beyond the traditional reliance on alliteration.

As for poetry, even before the Norman invasion rhyming had begun to replace alliteration as the distinguishing literary device of English verse. The influence of the French language furthered this development while also increasing the palette at the disposal of writers by introducing new words and different metres to the language. A significant example of a work which represents the developing sophistication of English poetry is *The Owl and the Nightingale*, written toward the end of the 12th century.

Arthurian legend had long been a popular topic for verse, and this remained true even after the Norman invasion. However, in the 13th century a movement toward long, didactic verse developed. These works focused on religious subjects or moral instruction. At the same time, verse romance was beginning to gain popularity, and this represented the development of a more commercially oriented form of writing. Meanwhile, another important development of this period was the emergence in English of lyric poetry. Often originally meant to be sung, lyric poems differ from verse romance thematically in that they centre on the expression of emotions rather than the telling of a story.

As time went on, the native English language had to grapple not only with the use of Anglo-Norman among the ruling classes and the persistent use of Latin by the educated classes but also with an increasing division into regional dialects. This division led to some localized literary trends, such as the revival of alliterative poetry in northern England. However, this revival was by no means a step backward, as 14th century works, such as *Winner and Waster*, *Piers Plowman*, and *Sir Gawayne* and the *Grene Knight,* show a linguistic sophistication and social consciousness not associated with older English works.

In the late 14th century the English language gained increasing acceptance in the royal court, especially during the reign of Richard II. The courtly poetry that was in fashion was not like the pointed tales of the alliterative revival, but rather centered on sentimental and romantic themes. Once again both the language itself and literary tastes were evolving in tandem, and this set the stage for the flowering of English literature which was to follow. Indeed, the Middle English period was about to produce English literature's first superstar.

Like many prominent figures in history Geoffrey Chaucer owed his success partly to talent and partly to being at the right place at the right time. As a man with a literary bent who spent time as a courtier and a diplomat, he was well positioned to capitalize on (and ultimately, expand) the popularity that English-language poetry was enjoying in the royal court during the late 14th century. Chaucer's writing reflects the changing times he lived in, for his early themes and styles borrowed heavily from popular French poetry. However, he soon moved beyond this to create a uniquely English body of work.

Stylistically, perhaps the most significant element of Chaucer's development was his fluid use of iambic pentameter. Thematically, Chaucer contributed heavily to the already-popular theme of courtly love, but in addition his use of narrative poetry expanded the story lines of English literature considerably. Also, his use of multiple narrators in his best-known work, The Canterbury Tales, unveils a technique that would still be considered challenging centuries later.

In part, Chaucer stands out so vividly in this period of English literature not only because he went beyond what his predecessors had accomplished, but also because the writers that followed him in the early 15th century failed to improve or build on what Chaucer had achieved. Works of this time were largely imitative of Chaucer and overly influenced by attempts to receive royal patronage.

Discussion of Middle English literature must focus largely on verse because there was no prose equivalent to the breakthrough represented by Chaucer. There were, however, the beginnings of an English dramatic tradition. Dramatic pieces of this period were typically either mystery cycles, which dealt with Biblical themes culminating in the Last Judgement, or morality plays such as *Everyman*. This foundation set the stage (literally and figuratively) for English drama to truly come of age during the subsequent Renaissance period.

Chronologically, the Renaissance period in English literature is considered to span from 1550 to 1660. Culturally, conditions were ripe for a boom period in literature due to a wide expansion of literacy in the preceding decades sparked by the introduction of printing to England in 1476. Meanwhile, social conditions were unsettled as the

English population expanded rapidly, creating an under-class of poor who often found no other place to turn than crime. Adding to this stormy backdrop was the Protestant Reformation, which was particularly violent in England because of the political dimension—Henry VIII had founded the Protestant Church of England, his daughter Queen Mary violently tried to restore Roman Catholicism to pre-eminence during her reign, and then Mary's half-sister, Elizabeth I, restored the Church of England but sought some measure of compromise.

Unsettled conditions often give rise to great art, and this period was no exception. The English language itself had come of age and was gaining acceptance as an alternative to classical languages, and soon the application of that vernacular would reach new heights. This was first evidenced in the writings of Sir Philip Sidney and Edmund Spenser, whose works exhibited a new facility with the English language and whose themes celebrated the value of beauty and artistry.

By this time, prose fiction had taken its place alongside poetry as a prominent and popular form of English literature. However, the form that really came of age during the Renaissance period of English literature was drama.

Going to the theatre achieved massive popularity during the reign of Elizabeth I, as everyone from the queen herself to common labourers enjoyed attending plays. With this popularity came the opportunity to make a substantial living as a playwright, which helped the craft attract the best writers of this generation. Or, in the case of William Shakespeare, perhaps the best writer of any generation.

Entire volumes have been filled with discussions of Shakespeare's works, but it is also instructive to consider him in the context of the development of English literature. Would a man of even Shakespeare's talents have reached such artistic heights and earned enduring fame had he been born a few centuries earlier? It seems that the development of the language and the popularity of poetry and the theatre primed conditions for Shakespeare to make the most of his talents.

Those talents were evident in both form and substance. An accomplished poet and playwright, Shakespeare's best dramatic works melded the two forms into powerful storytelling using language that is by turns lyrical and chilling but most of all memorable. As for the stories, it is the complexity of Shakespeare's characterizations that have inspired subsequent centuries' worth of study and debate. These are no longer the one-dimensional heroes and villains of Old English tales, but rather multifaceted personalities with elements of both good and evil. As remarkable as his use of language is, it is perhaps the psychology of Shakespeare's writing—generations before psychology became a formal field of study—that has had the greatest influence on literature, right up to the present day.

Shakespeare's star shone so brightly that it would be easy to overlook the other lights of the Renaissance era in English literature, but this would be unfortunate. Shakespeare's contemporary Christopher Marlowe also elevated the dramatic form by using his characters to explore the internal and external workings of power and greed. Another contemporary, Ben Jonson, used humour as his weapon against the ills of society, a technique that remains vibrant today. A generation later, in the mid-17th century, John Milton used his poetry not simply for social commentary but in an effort to influence events.

By Milton's time, the landscape for English literature had become somewhat fractured. Whereas so many elements had seemed to come together during the Elizabethan period, both artistic and political divisions appeared during the subsequent reign of the Stuarts in England, which began in 1603. A rift developed between popular theatre and the more stylized plays of court society. By the 1640s, political tensions would explode into the English Civil War, which temporarily did away with the monarchy (and permanently did away with one monarch, Charles I). Clearly times were ripe for a change in all aspects of English life, and literature was no exception. The Renaissance period was over, but the growth of English literature was not. Already an extraordinary standard had been set.

As this volume will detail, the evolution of literature from the Old English period through the Renaissance represents a change that seems staggering to this day. In the process, a language and culture assimilated diverse influences, and the art which resulted both defined its times and, in some cases, became timeless.

CHAPTER 1

THE OLD ENGLISH PERIOD

English literature, defined here as the body of written works produced in the English language by inhabitants of the British Isles (including Ireland) from the 7th century to the present day, has sometimes been stigmatized as insular. It can be argued that no single English novel attains the universality of the Russian writer Leo Tolstoy's *War and Peace* or the French writer Gustave Flaubert's *Madame Bovary*. Yet in the Middle Ages the Old English literature of the subjugated Saxons was leavened by the Latin and Anglo-Norman writings, eminently foreign in origin, in which the churchmen and the Norman conquerors expressed themselves. From this combination emerged a flexible and subtle linguistic instrument exploited by Geoffrey Chaucer and brought to supreme application by William Shakespeare. During the Renaissance the renewed interest in Classical learning and values had an important effect on English literature, as on all the arts. Ideas of Augustan literary propriety in the 18th century and reverence in the 19th century for a less specific, though still selectively viewed, Classical antiquity continued to shape the literature. All three of these impulses derived from a foreign source, namely the Mediterranean basin. The Decadents of the late 19th century and the Modernists of the early 20th looked to continental European individuals and movements for inspiration. Nor was attraction toward European intellectualism dead in the late 20th century, for by the mid-1980s the approach known as structuralism, a phenomenon predominantly French and German in origin, infused the very study of English literature itself in a host of published critical studies and university departments. Additional influence was exercised by deconstructionist analysis, based largely on the work of French philosopher Jacques Derrida.

Further, Britain's past imperial activities around the globe continued to inspire literature—in some cases wistful, in other cases hostile. Finally, English literature has enjoyed a certain diffusion abroad, not only in predominantly English-speaking countries but also in all those others where English is the first choice of study as a second language.

English literature is therefore not so much insular as detached from the continental European tradition across the Channel. It is strong in all the conventional categories of the bookseller's list: in Shakespeare it has a dramatist of world renown; in poetry, a genre notoriously resistant to adequate translation and therefore difficult to compare with the poetry of other literatures, it is so peculiarly rich as to merit inclusion in the front rank; English literature's humour has been found as hard to convey to foreigners as poetry, if not more so—a fact at any rate permitting bestowal of the label "idiosyncratic"; English literature's remarkable body of travel writings constitutes another counterthrust to the charge of insularity; in autobiography, biography, and historical writing, English literature compares with the best of any culture; and children's literature, fantasy, essays, and journals, which tend to be considered minor genres, are all fields of exceptional achievement as regards English literature. Even in philosophical writings, popularly thought of as hard to combine with literary value, thinkers such as Thomas Hobbes, John Locke, David Hume, John Stuart Mill, and Bertrand Russell stand comparison for lucidity and grace with the best of the French philosophers and the masters of Classical antiquity.

Some of English literature's most distinguished practitioners in the 20th century—from Joseph Conrad at its beginning to V.S. Naipaul and Tom Stoppard at its end—were born outside the British Isles. What is more, none of the aforementioned had as much in common with his adoptive country as did, for instance, Doris Lessing and Peter Porter (two other distinguished writer-immigrants to Britain), both having been born into a British family and having been brought up on British Commonwealth soil.

On the other hand, during the same period in the 20th century, many notable practitioners of English literature left the British Isles to live abroad: James Joyce, D.H. Lawrence, Aldous Huxley, Christopher Isherwood, Robert Graves, Graham Greene, Muriel Spark, and Anthony Burgess. In one case, that of Samuel Beckett, this process was carried to the extent of writing works first in French and then translating them into English.

Even English literature considered purely as a product of the British Isles is extraordinarily heterogeneous, however. Literature actually written in those Celtic tongues once prevalent in Cornwall, Ireland, Scotland, and Wales—called the "Celtic Fringe"—is treated separately. Yet Irish, Scots, and Welsh writers have contributed enormously to English literature even when they have written in dialect, as the 18th-century poet Robert Burns and the 20th-century Scots writer Alasdair Gray have done. In the latter half of the 20th century, interest began also to focus on writings in English or English dialect by recent settlers in Britain, such as Afro-Caribbeans and people from Africa proper, the Indian subcontinent, and East Asia.

Even within England, culturally and historically the dominant partner in the union of territories comprising Britain, literature has been as enriched by strongly provincial writers as by metropolitan ones. Another contrast more fruitful than not for English letters has been that between social milieus, however much observers of Britain in their own writings may have deplored the survival of class distinctions. As far back as medieval times, a courtly tradition in literature cross-fertilized with an earthier demotic one. Shakespeare's frequent juxtaposition of royalty in one scene with plebeians in the next reflects a very British way of looking at society. This awareness of differences between high life and low, a state of affairs fertile in creative tensions, is observable throughout the history of English literature.

POETRY

Virtually all Old English poetry is written in a single metre, a four-stress line with a syntactical break, or caesura, between the second and third stresses, and with alliteration linking the two halves of the line. This pattern is occasionally varied by six-stress lines. The poetry is formulaic, drawing on a common set of stock phrases and phrase patterns, applying standard epithets to various classes of characters, and depicting scenery with such recurring images as the eagle and the wolf, which wait during battles to feast on carrion, and ice and snow, which appear in the landscape to signal sorrow. In the best poems such formulas, far from being tedious, give a strong impression of the richness of the cultural fund from which poets could draw. Other standard devices of this poetry are the kenning, a figurative name for a thing, usually expressed in a compound noun (e.g., *swan-road* used to name the sea); and variation, the repeating of a single idea in different words, with each repetition adding a new level of meaning. That these verse techniques changed little during 400 years of literary production suggests the extreme conservatism of Anglo-Saxon culture.

The Major Manuscripts

Most Old English poetry is preserved in four manuscripts of the late 10th and early 11th centuries. The Beowulf Manuscript (British Library) contains *Beowulf*, *Judith*, and three prose tracts; the Exeter Book (Exeter Cathedral) is a miscellaneous gathering of lyrics, riddles, didactic poems, and religious narratives; the Junius Manuscript (Bodleian Library, Oxford)—also called the Caedmon Manuscript, even though its contents are no longer attributed to Caedmon—contains biblical paraphrases; and the Vercelli Book (found in the cathedral library in Vercelli, Italy) contains saints' lives, several short religious poems, and prose homilies. In addition to the poems in these books are historical poems in the *Anglo-Saxon Chronicle*; poetic renderings of Psalms 51–150; the 31 *Metres* included in King Alfred the Great's translation of Boethius's *De consolatione philosophiae* (*Consolation of Philosophy*); magical, didactic, elegiac, and heroic poems; and others, miscellaneously interspersed with prose, jotted in margins, and even worked in stone or metal.

PROBLEMS OF DATING

Few poems can be dated as closely as Caedmon's "Hymn". King Alfred's compositions fall into the late 9th century, and Bede composed his "Death Song" within 50 days of his death on May 25, 735. Historical poems such as "The Battle of Brunanburh" (after 937) and *The Battle of Maldon* (after 991) are fixed by the dates of the events they commemorate. A translation of one of Aldhelm's riddles is found not only in the Exeter Book but also in an early 9th-century manuscript at Leiden, Neth. And at least a part of "The Dream of the Rood" can be dated by an excerpt carved on the 8th-century Ruthwell Cross (in Dumfriesshire, Scot.). But in the absence of such indications, Old English poems are hard to date, and the scholarly consensus that most were composed in the Midlands and the North in the 8th and 9th centuries gave way to uncertainty during the last two decades of the 20th century. Many now hold that "The Wanderer," *Beowulf*, and other poems once assumed to have been written in the 8th century are of the 9th century or later. For most poems, there is no scholarly consensus beyond the belief that they were written between the 8th and the 11th centuries.

RELIGIOUS VERSE

If few poems can be dated accurately, still fewer can be attributed to particular poets. The most important author from whom a considerable body of work survives is Cynewulf, who wove his runic signature into the epilogues of four poems. Aside from his name, little is known of him. He probably lived in the 9th century in Mercia or Northumbria. His works include *The Fates of the Apostles*, a short martyrology; *The Ascension* (also called *Christ II*), a homily and biblical narrative; *Juliana*, a saint's passion set in the reign of the Roman emperor Maximian (late 3rd century CE); and *Elene*, perhaps the best of his poems, which describes the mission of St. Helena, mother of the emperor Constantine, to recover Christ's cross. Cynewulf's work is lucid and technically elegant. His theme is the continuing evangelical mission from the time of Christ to the triumph of Christianity under Constantine. Several poems not by Cynewulf are associated with him because of their subject matter. These include two lives of St. Guthlac and *Andreas*. The latter, the apocryphal story of how St. Andrew fell into the hands of the cannibalistic (and presumably mythical) Mermedonians, has stylistic affinities with *Beowulf*. Also in the "Cynewulf group" are several poems with Christ as their subject, of which the most important is 'The Dream of the Rood," in which the cross speaks of itself as Christ's loyal thane and yet the instrument of his death. This tragic paradox echoes a recurring theme of secular poetry and at the same time movingly expresses the religious paradoxes of Christ's triumph in death and humankind's redemption from sin.

Several poems of the Junius Manuscript are based on the Old Testament narratives Genesis, Exodus, and Daniel. Of these, *Exodus* is remarkable for its intricate diction and bold imagery. The fragmentary *Judith* of the Beowulf Manuscript stirringly embellishes the story from the Apocrypha of the heroine who led the Jews to victory over the Assyrians.

ELEGIAC AND HEROIC VERSE

The term *elegy* is used of Old English poems that lament the loss of worldly goods, glory, or human companionship. "The Wanderer" is narrated by a man, deprived of lord and kinsmen, whose journeys lead him to the realization that there is stability only in heaven. "The Seafarer" is similar, but its journey motif more explicitly symbolizes the speaker's spiritual yearnings. Several others have similar themes, and three elegies—"The Husband's Message," "The Wife's Lament," and "Wulf and Eadwacer"—describe what appears to be a conventional situation: the separation of husband and wife by the husband's exile.

"Deor" bridges the gap between the elegy and the heroic poem, for in it a poet laments the loss of his position at court by alluding to sorrowful stories from Germanic legend. *Beowulf* itself narrates the battles of Beowulf, a prince of the Geats (a tribe in what is now southern Sweden), against the monstrous Grendel, Grendel's mother, and a fire-breathing dragon. The account contains some of the best elegiac verse in the language, and, by setting marvelous tales against a historical background in which victory is always temporary and strife is always renewed, the poet gives the whole an elegiac cast. *Beowulf* also is one of the best religious poems, not only because of its explicitly Christian passages but also because Beowulf's monstrous foes are depicted as God's enemies and Beowulf

An illustration of the battle of Brunanburh by Alfred Pearse. Included in the Anglo-Saxon Chronicle, the poem "The Battle of Brunanburh" details the Saxon victories over invaders. Private Collection/The Stapleton Collection/ The Bridgeman Art Library

himself as God's champion. Other heroic narratives are fragmentary. Of *The Battle of Finnsburh* and *Waldere* only enough remains to indicate that, when whole, they must have been fast-paced and stirring.

Of several poems dealing with English history and preserved in the *Anglo-Saxon Chronicle*, the most notable is "The Battle of Brunanburh," a panegyric on the occasion of King Athelstan's victory over a coalition of Norsemen and Scots in 937.

But the best historical poem is not from the *Anglo-Saxon Chronicle*. *The Battle of Maldon*, which describes the defeat of Aldorman Byrhtnoth and much of his army at the hands of Viking invaders in 991, discovers in defeat an occasion to celebrate the heroic ideal, contrasting the determination of many of Byrhtnoth's thanes to avenge his death or die in the attempt with the cowardice of others who left the field. Minor poetic genres include catalogs (two sets of *Maxims* and *Widsith*, a list of rulers, tribes, and notables in the heroic age), dialogues, metrical prefaces and epilogues to prose works of the Alfredian period, and liturgical poems associated with the Benedictine Office.

PROSE

The earliest English prose work, the law code of King Aethelberht I of Kent, was written within a few years of the arrival in England (597) of St. Augustine of Canterbury. Other 7th- and 8th-century prose, similarly practical in character, includes more laws, wills, and charters. According to Cuthbert, who was a monk at Jarrow, Bede at the time of his death had just finished a translation of the Gospel of St. John, though this does not survive. Two medical tracts, *Herbarium* and *Medicina de quadrupedibus*, very likely date from the 8th century.

EARLY TRANSLATIONS INTO ENGLISH

The earliest literary prose dates from the late 9th century, when King Alfred, eager to improve the state of English learning, led a vigorous program to translate into English "certain books that are necessary for all men to know." Alfred himself translated the *Pastoral Care* of St. Gregory I the Great, the *Consolation of Philosophy* of Boethius, the *Soliloquies* of St. Augustine of Hippo, and the first 50 Psalms. His *Pastoral Care* is a fairly literal translation, but his Boethius is extensively restructured and revised to

King Alfred led an effort to translate texts into the English language. Alfred himself translated a number of manuscripts, including the first 50 Psalms of the Bible. Hulton Archive/Getty Images

make explicit the Christian message that medieval commentators saw in that work. He revised the *Soliloquies* even more radically, departing from his source to draw from Gregory and St. Jerome, as well as from other works by Augustine. Alfred's prefaces to these works are of great historical interest.

At Alfred's urging, Bishop Werferth of Worcester translated the *Dialogues* of Gregory. Probably Alfred also inspired anonymous scholars to translate Bede's *Historia ecclesiastica gentis Anglorum* (*Ecclesiastical History of the English People*) and Paulus Orosius's *Historiarum adversum paganos libri vii* (*Seven Books of History Against the Pagans*). Both of these works are much abridged. The Bede translation follows its source slavishly, but the translator of Orosius added many details of northern European geography and also accounts of the voyages of Ohthere the Norwegian and Wulfstan the Dane. These accounts, in addition to their geographical interest, show that friendly commerce between England and Scandinavia was possible even during the Danish wars. *The Anglo-Saxon Chronicle* probably originated in Alfred's reign. Its earliest annals (beginning in the reign of Julius Caesar) are laconic, except the entry for 755, which records in detail a feud between the West Saxon king Cynewulf and the would-be usurper Cyneheard.

The entries covering the Danish wars of the late 9th century are much fuller, and those running from the reign of Ethelred II to the Norman Conquest in 1066 (when *The Anglo-Saxon Chronicle* exists in several versions) contain many passages of excellent writing. The early 10th century is not notable for literary production, but some of the homilies in the Vercelli Book and the Blickling Manuscript (Scheide Library, Princeton University) may belong to that period.

LATE 10TH- AND 11TH-CENTURY PROSE

The prose literature of the mid- to late 10th century is associated with the Benedictine Reform, a movement that sought to impose order and discipline on a monastic establishment that was thought to have grown lax. Aethelwold, bishop of Winchester and one of the leaders of the reform, translated the Rule of St. Benedict. But the greatest and most prolific writer of this period was his pupil Aelfric, a monk at Cerne and later abbot of Eynsham, whose works include three cycles of 40 homilies each (*Catholic Homilies*, 2 vol., and the *Lives of the Saints*), as well as homilies not in these cycles; a Latin grammar; a treatise on time and natural history; pastoral letters; and several translations. His Latin *Colloquy*, supplied with an Old English version by an anonymous glossarist, gives a fascinating glimpse into the Anglo-Saxon monastic classroom. Aelfric wrote with lucidity and astonishing beauty, using the rhetorical devices of Latin literature frequently but without ostentation. His later alliterative prose, which loosely imitates the rhythms of Old English poetry, influenced writers long after the Norman Conquest.

In addition, Wulfstan, archbishop of York, wrote legal codes, both civil and ecclesiastical, and a number of homilies, including *Sermo Lupi ad Anglos* ("Wulf's Address to the English"), a ferocious denunciation of the morals of his time. To judge from the number of extant manuscripts, both he and Aelfric were enormously popular.

Byrhtferth of Ramsey wrote several Latin works and the *Enchiridion*, a textbook on the calendar notable for its ornate style. Numerous anonymous works, some of very high quality, were produced in this period, including homilies, saints' lives, dialogues, and translations of such works as the Gospels, several Old Testament books, liturgical texts, monastic rules, penitential handbooks, and the romance *Apollonius of Tyre* (translated from Latin but probably derived from a Greek original).

The works of the Benedictine Reform were written during a few remarkable decades around the turn of the millennium. Little original work can be securely dated to the period after Wulfstan's death (1023), but the continued vigour of *The Anglo-Saxon Chronicle* shows that good Old English prose was written right up to the Norman Conquest.

SIGNIFICANT FIGURES AND TEXTS

Scholars know relatively little about most of the writers of the Old English period, and what is known is often deduced from the fragmentary manuscripts that survive from the era. The following highlights some of the notable writers and texts during this time.

NOTABLE OLD ENGLISH WRITERS

The Anglo-Saxon theologian and historian Bede is perhaps the most important and most prolific writer of the period, and his dating of historical events from Christ's birth gained universal use in the West for centuries. By contrast, the poet called Cynewulf is known as such only by way of an acrostic. No other biographical information is known. The works of both, however—as well as those of the other writers noted in this section—provide much insight into their era.

AELFRIC
(fl. *c.* 955–*c.* 1025, probably Eynsham, Oxfordshire, Eng.)

Aelfric was an Anglo-Saxon prose writer, considered the greatest of his time. He wrote both to instruct the monks

and to spread the learning of the 10th-century monastic revival. His *Catholic Homilies,* written in 990–92, provided orthodox sermons, based on the Church Fathers. Author of a Latin grammar, hence his nickname Grammaticus, he also wrote *Lives of the Saints, Heptateuch* (a vernacular language version of the first seven books of the Bible), as well as letters and various treatises.

CAEDMON
(fl. 658–680)

Caedmon was the first Old English Christian poet. His fragmentary hymn to the creation remains a symbol of the adaptation of the aristocratic-heroic Anglo-Saxon verse tradition to the expression of Christian themes. His story is known from Bede's *Ecclesiastical History of the English People,* which tells how Caedmon, an illiterate herdsman, retired from company one night in shame because he could not comply with the demand made of each guest to sing. Then in a dream a stranger appeared commanding him to sing of "the beginning of things," and the herdsman found himself uttering "verses which he had never heard." When Caedmon awoke he related his dream to the farm bailiff under whom he worked and was conducted by him to the monastery at Streaneshalch (now called Whitby). The abbess St. Hilda believed that Caedmon was divinely inspired and, to test his powers, proposed that he should render into verse a portion of sacred history, which the monks explained. By the following morning he had fulfilled the task. At the request of the abbess, he became an inmate of the monastery.

Throughout the remainder of his life, his more learned brethren expounded Scripture to him, and all that he heard he reproduced in vernacular poetry. All of his poetry was on sacred themes, and its unvarying aim was to turn men from sin to righteousness. In spite of all the poetic renderings that Caedmon supposedly made, however, it is only the original dream hymn of nine historically precious, but poetically uninspired, lines that can be attributed to him with confidence. The hymn—extant in 17 manuscripts, some in the poet's Northumbrian dialect, some in other Old English dialects — set the pattern for almost the whole art of Anglo-Saxon verse.

CYNEWULF
(fl. 9th century ad, Northumbria or Mercia [now in England])

Cynewulf, whose name is sometimes spelled Cynwulf or Kynewulf, is considered the author of four Old English poems preserved in late 10th-century manuscripts. *Elene* and *The Fates of the Apostles* are in the Vercelli Book, and *The Ascension* (which forms the second part of a trilogy, *Christ,* and is also called *Christ II*) and *Juliana* are in the Exeter Book. An epilogue to each poem, asking for prayers for the author, contains runic characters representing the letters *c, y, n, (e), w, u, l, f,* which are thought to spell his name. A rhymed passage in the *Elene* shows that Cynewulf wrote in the Northumbrian or Mercian dialect. Nothing is known of him outside his poems, as there is no reason to identify him with any of the recorded persons bearing this common name. He may have been a learned cleric since all of the poems are based on Latin sources.

Elene, a poem of 1,321 lines, is an account of the finding of the True Cross by St. Helena. *The Fates of the Apostles,* at 122 lines, is a versified martyrology describing the mission and death of each of the Twelve Apostles. *Christ II (The Ascension)* is a lyrical version of a homily on the Ascension written by Pope Gregory I the Great. It is part of a trilogy on Christ by different authors. *Juliana,* a poem of 731 lines, is a retelling of a Latin prose life of St. Juliana, a maiden who rejected the suit of a Roman prefect, Eleusius, because of her faith and consequently was made to suffer numerous torments.

Although the poems do not have great power or originality, they are more than mere paraphrases. Imagery from everyday Old English life and from the Germanic epic tradition enlivens descriptions of battles and sea voyages. At the same time, the poet, a careful and skillful craftsman, consciously applies the principles of Latin rhetoric to achieve a clarity and orderly narrative progress that is quite unlike the confusion and circumlocution of the native English style.

SAINT BEDE THE VENERABLE

(b. 672/673, traditionally Monkton in Jarrow, Northumbria [now in England] — d. May 25, 735, Jarrow; canonized 1899; feast day May 25)

Saint Bede the Venerable was an Anglo-Saxon theologian, historian, and chronologist best known today for his *Ecclesiastical History of the English People*, a source vital to the history of the conversion to Christianity of the Anglo-Saxon tribes. During his lifetime and throughout the Middle Ages Bede's reputation was based mainly on his scriptural commentaries, copies of which found their way to many of the monastic libraries of western Europe. His method of dating events from the time of the incarnation, or Christ's birth — i.e., AD — came into general use through the popularity of the *Ecclesiastical History* and the two works on chronology. Bede's influence was perpetuated at home through the school founded at York by his pupil Archbishop Egbert of York and was transmitted to the Continent by Alcuin, who studied there before becoming master of Charlemagne's palace school at Aachen.

Nothing is known of Bede's parentage. At the age of seven he was taken to the Monastery of St. Peter, founded at Wearmouth (near Sunderland, Durham) by Abbot St. Benedict Biscop, to whose care he was entrusted. By 685 he was moved to Biscop's newer Monastery of St. Paul at Jarrow. Bede (also spelled as Baeda or Beda) was ordained deacon when 19 years old and priest when 30. Apart from

*Saint Bede the Venerable was known during his lifetime for writing scriptural
commentaries, but he is today renowned for his* Ecclesiastical History of
the English People, *a crucial piece of Christian history.* Kean Collection/
Hulton Archive/Getty Images

visits to Lindisfarne and York, he seems never to have left
Wearmouth–Jarrow. Buried at Jarrow, his remains were
removed to Durham and are now entombed in the Galilee
Chapel of Durham Cathedral.

Bede's works fall into three groups: grammatical and
"scientific," scriptural commentary, and historical and
biographical. His earliest works include treatises on spelling, hymns, figures of speech, verse, and epigrams. His
first treatise on chronology, *De temporibus* ("On Times"),
with a brief chronicle attached, was written in 703. In 725
he completed a greatly amplified version, *De temporum
ratione* ("On the Reckoning of Time"), with a much longer

chronicle. Both these books were mainly concerned with the reckoning of Easter. His earliest biblical commentary was probably that on the Revelation to John (703?–709). In this and many similar works, his aim was to transmit and explain relevant passages from the Fathers of the Church. Although his interpretations were mainly allegorical, treating much of the biblical text as symbolic of deeper meanings, he used some critical judgment and attempted to rationalize discrepancies. Among his most notable are his verse (705–716) and prose (before 721) lives of St. Cuthbert, bishop of Lindisfarne. These works are uncritical and abound with accounts of miracles. A more exclusively historical work is *Historia abbatum* (*c.* 725; "Lives of the Abbots").

In 731/732 Bede completed his *Ecclesiastical History.* Divided into five books, it recorded events in Britain from the raids by Julius Caesar (55–54 BCE) to the arrival in Kent (597 CE) of St. Augustine. For his sources he claimed the authority of ancient letters, the "traditions of our forefathers," and his own knowledge of contemporary events. Bede's *Ecclesiastical History* leaves gaps tantalizing to secular historians. Although overloaded with the miraculous, it is the work of a scholar anxious to assess the accuracy of his sources and to record only what he regarded as trustworthy evidence. It remains an indispensable source for some of the facts and much of the feel of early Anglo-Saxon history.

NOTABLE OLD ENGLISH TEXTS

Beowulf is the greatest monument of Old English literature. Its story of the prince Beowulf and the monster Grendel still captivates readers today; a translation into modern English by the Irish poet Seamus Heaney became an international best seller at the turn of the 21st century.

Yet other texts, in prose and in verse, are just as important to understanding the period during which they were written.

ANGLO-SAXON CHRONICLE

The *Anglo-Saxon Chronicle*, a chronological account of events in Anglo-Saxon and Norman England, is a compilation of seven surviving interrelated manuscript records that is the primary source for the early history of England. The narrative was first assembled in the reign of King Alfred (871–899) from materials that included some epitome of universal history: Bede's *Ecclesiastical History*, genealogies, regnal and episcopal lists, a few northern annals, and probably some sets of earlier West Saxon annals. The compiler also had access to a set of Frankish annals for the late 9th century.

Soon after the year 890, several manuscripts were being circulated. One was available to Asser in 893, another, which appears to have gone no further than that year, to the late 10th-century chronicler Aethelweard, while one version, which eventually reached the north, stopped in 892. Some of the manuscripts circulated at this time were continued in various religious houses, sometimes with annals that occur in more than one manuscript, sometimes with local material, confined to one version. The fullness and quality of the entries vary at different periods. The *Chronicle* is a rather barren document for the mid-10th century and for the reign of Canute, for example, but it is an excellent authority for the reign of Aethelred the Unready and from the reign of Edward the Confessor until the version that was kept up longest ends with annal 1154. The *Chronicle* survived to the modern period in seven manuscripts (one of these being destroyed in the 18th century) and a fragment, which are generally known by letters of the alphabet.

"THE BATTLE OF BRUNANBURH"

"The Battle of Brunanburh" is an Old English poem of 73 lines included in the Anglo-Saxon Chronicle under the year 937. As previously mentioned, it relates the victory of the Saxon king Athelstan over the allied Norse, Scots, and Strathclyde Briton invaders under the leadership of Olaf Guthfrithson, king of Dublin and claimant to the throne of York. The poem is probably a panegyric composed for Athelstan to celebrate his victory. It counts the dead kings and earls on the battlefield and pictures the Norsemen slinking back to Dublin in their ships while their dead sons are being devoured by ravens and wolves. The poem claims that this was the greatest battle ever fought in England.

THE BATTLE OF MALDON

The Battle of Maldon is an Old English heroic poem describing a historical skirmish between East Saxons and Viking (mainly Norwegian) raiders in 991. It is incomplete, its beginning and ending both lost. The poem is remarkable for its vivid, dramatic combat scenes and for its expression of the Germanic ethos of loyalty to a leader.

The poem, as it survives, opens with the war parties aligned on either side of a stream (the present River Blackwater near Maldon, Essex). The Vikings offer the cynical suggestion that the English may buy their peace with golden rings. The English commander Earl Byrhtnoth replies that they will pay their tribute in spears and darts. When the Vikings cannot advance because of their poor position, Byrhtnoth recklessly allows them safe conduct across the stream, and the battle follows. In spite of Byrhtnoth's supreme feats of courage, he is finally slain. In panic some of the English warriors desert. The names of the deserters are carefully recorded in the poem along with the names and genealogies of the loyal retainers who stand fast to avenge Byrhtnoth's death. The 325-line fragment ends with the rallying speech of the old warrior Byrhtwold (here in modern English):

Mind must be firmer, heart the more fierce,
Courage the greater, as our strength
diminishes ....

BEOWULF

The heroic poem *Beowulf* is the highest achievement of Old English literature and the earliest European vernacular epic. Preserved in a single manuscript (Cotton Vitellius A XV) from *c.* 1000, it deals with events of the early 6th century and is believed to have been composed between 700 and 750. It did not appear in print until 1815. Although originally untitled, it was later named after the Scandinavian hero Beowulf, whose exploits and character provide its connecting theme. There is no evidence of a historical Beowulf, but some characters, sites, and events in the poem can be historically verified.

The poem falls into two parts. It opens in Denmark, where King Hrothgar's splendid mead hall, Heorot, has been ravaged for 12 years by nightly visits from an evil monster, Grendel, who carries off Hrothgar's warriors and devours them. Unexpectedly, young Beowulf, a prince of the Geats of southern Sweden, arrives with a small band of retainers and offers to cleanse Heorot of its monster. The King is astonished at the little-known hero's daring but welcomes him, and after an evening of feasting, much courtesy, and some discourtesy, the King retires, leaving Beowulf in charge. During the night Grendel comes from the moors, tears open the heavy doors, and devours one of the sleeping Geats. He then grapples with Beowulf, whose

The only extant manuscript of the heroic poem Beowulf—considered the greatest Old English epic—is housed in the British Museum. Hulton Archive/ Getty Images

powerful grip he cannot escape. Grendel wrenches himself free, tearing off his arm, and leaves, mortally wounded.

The next day is one of rejoicing in Heorot. But at night as the warriors sleep, Grendel's mother comes to avenge her son, killing one of Hrothgar's men. In the morning Beowulf seeks her out in her cave at the bottom of a mere and kills her. He cuts the head from Grendel's corpse and returns to Heorot. The Danes rejoice once more. Hrothgar makes a farewell speech about the character of the true hero, as Beowulf, enriched with honours and princely gifts, returns home to King Hygelac of the Geats.

The second part passes rapidly over King Hygelac's subsequent death in a battle (of historical record), the death of his son, and Beowulf's succession to the kingship and his peaceful rule of 50 years. But now a fire-breathing dragon ravages his land and the doughty but aging Beowulf engages it. The fight is long and terrible and a painful contrast to the battles of his youth. Painful, too, is the desertion of his retainers except for his young kinsman Wiglaf. Beowulf kills the dragon but is mortally wounded. The poem ends with his funeral rites and a lament.

Beowulf belongs metrically, stylistically, and thematically to the inherited Germanic heroic tradition. Many incidents, such as Beowulf's tearing off the monster's arm and his descent into the mere, are familiar motifs from folklore. The ethical values are manifestly the Germanic code of loyalty to chief and tribe and vengeance to enemies. Yet the poem is so infused with a Christian spirit that it lacks the grim fatality of many of the Eddic lays or the Icelandic sagas. Beowulf himself seems more altruistic than other Germanic heroes or the heroes of the *Iliad*. It is significant that his three battles are not against men, which would entail the retaliation of the blood feud, but against evil monsters, enemies of the whole community and of civilization itself. Many critics have seen the poem as a Christian allegory, with Beowulf the champion of goodness and light against the forces of evil and darkness. His sacrificial death is not seen as tragic but as the fitting end of a good (some would say "too good") hero's life.

That is not to say that *Beowulf* is an optimistic poem. The English critic J.R.R. Tolkien suggests that its total effect is more like a long, lyrical elegy than an epic. Even the earlier, happier section in Denmark is filled with ominous allusions that were well understood by contemporary audiences. Thus, after Grendel's death, King Hrothgar speaks sanguinely of the future, which the audience knows will end with the destruction of his line and the burning of Heorot. In the second part the movement is slow and funereal. Scenes from Beowulf's youth are replayed in a minor key as a counterpoint to his last battle, and the mood becomes increasingly sombre as the *wyrd* (fate) that comes to all men closes in on him.

"DEOR"

Deor, a *scop* (minstrel), is the narrator of the Old English heroic poem of 42 lines known as "Deor", which is one of the two surviving Old English poems to have a refrain. (The other is the fragmentary "Wulf and Eadwacer.") The poem, which is also sometimes called "Deor's Lament", is the complaint of Deor, who was replaced at his court by another minstrel and deprived of his lands and his lord's favour. In the poem Deor recalls, in irregular stanzas, five examples of the sufferings of various figures from Germanic legend. Each stanza ends with the refrain "That trouble passed; so can this." Though some scholars believe that the lament is merely a conventional pretext for introducing heroic legends, and thus that Deor is not a historical figure, the mood of the poem remains intensely personal.

"THE DREAM OF THE ROOD"

"The Dream of the Rood" is an Old English lyric, the earliest dream poem and one of the finest religious poems in the English language, once, but no longer, attributed to Caedmon or Cynewulf. In a dream the unknown poet beholds a beautiful tree—the rood, or cross, on which Christ died. The rood tells him its own story. Forced to be the instrument of the saviour's death, it describes how it suffered the nail wounds, spear shafts, and insults along with Christ to fulfill God's will. Once blood-stained and horrible, it is now the resplendent sign of mankind's redemption. The poem was originally known only in fragmentary form from some 8th-century runic inscriptions on the Ruthwell Cross, now standing in the parish church of Ruthwell, now Dumfries District, Dumfries and Galloway Region, Scot. The complete version became known with the discovery of the 10th-century Vercelli Book in northern Italy in 1822.

EXETER BOOK

The Exeter Book is the largest extant collection of Old English poetry. Copied *c.* 975, the manuscript was given to Exeter Cathedral by Bishop Leofric (d. 1072). It begins with some long religious poems: the *Christ,* in three parts; two poems on St. Guthlac; the fragmentary "Azarius"; and the allegorical *Phoenix.* Following these are a number of shorter religious verses intermingled with poems of types that have survived only in this codex. All the extant Anglo-Saxon lyrics, or elegies, as they are usually called—"The Wanderer," "The Seafarer," "The Wife's Lament," "The Husband's Message," and "The Ruin"—are found here. These are secular poems evoking a poignant sense of desolation and loneliness in their descriptions of the separation of lovers, the sorrows of exile, or the terrors and attractions of the sea, although some of them—e.g., "The Wanderer" and "The Seafarer"—also carry the weight of religious allegory. In addition, the Exeter Book preserves 95 riddles, a genre that would otherwise have been represented by a solitary example.

The remaining part of the Exeter Book includes "The Rhyming Poem," which is the only example of its kind; the gnomic verses; "Widsith," the heroic narrative of a fictitious bard; and the two refrain poems, "Deor" and "Wulf and Eadwacer." The arrangement of the poems appears to be haphazard, and the book is believed to be copied from an earlier collection.

"THE HUSBAND'S MESSAGE"

"The Husband's Message" is an Old English lyric preserved in the Exeter Book, one of the few surviving love lyrics from the Anglo-Saxon period. It is remarkable for its ingenious form and for its emotive power. The speaker is a wooden staff on which a message from an exiled husband to his wife has been carved in runic letters. The staff tells how it grew as a sapling beside the sea, never dreaming it would have the power of speech, until a man carved a secret message on it. The husband's message tells of how he was forced to flee because of a feud but now has wealth and power in a new land and longs for his wife. It implores her to set sail and join him.

JUNIUS MANUSCRIPT

The Junius Manuscript consists of Old English scriptural paraphrases copied about 1000, given in 1651 to the scholar Franciscus Junius by Archbishop James Ussher of Armagh and now in the Bodleian Library, University of Oxford. It contains the poems *Genesis, Exodus, Daniel,* and *Christ and*

Satan, originally attributed to Caedmon because these subjects correspond roughly to the subjects described in Bede's *Ecclesiastical History* as having been rendered by Caedmon into vernacular verse. The whole, called Caedmon's Paraphrase, was first published in 1655. The manuscript itself is also called the Caedmon Manuscript, although studies have made the attribution to Caedmon doubtful, because the poems seem to have been written at different periods and by more than one author.

Genesis is a poem of 2,936 lines. The first 234 lines describe the fall of angels and parts of the creation. Lines 235–851 give a second account of the fall of angels and tell of the fall of man. The sequence, style, and superior quality of these lines reveal them to be interpolated. This section, later identified as a translation of an Old Saxon original, is now known as Genesis B. Its many striking resemblances to *Paradise Lost* suggest that John Milton might have known of the manuscript. The remaining portions, Genesis A, carry the story up to the sacrifice of Isaac.

Exodus, an incomplete poem of 590 lines regarded as older than *Genesis* or *Daniel,* describes the flight of the Israelites with considerable dramatic power.

Daniel, an incomplete poem of 764 lines, is a scholarly work closely following the Vulgate Book of Daniel and much inferior to *Exodus* in poetic quality.

The 729-line piece known as *Christ and Satan* contains a lament of the fallen angels, a description of the harrowing of hell (Christ's descent into hell after his death), and an account of the temptation of Christ by Satan. In spite of its anachronistic sequence, it is regarded by some scholars as a single poem, its unifying theme being the "sufferings of Satan." It has a rude vigour and lack of culture and polish. The manuscript also contains drawings.

VERCELLI BOOK

The Vercelli Book (Latin: Codex Vercellensis) is an Old English manuscript written in the late 10th century. It contains texts of the poem *Andreas,* two poems by Cynewulf, "The Dream of the Rood," an "Address of the Saved Soul to the Body," and a fragment of a homiletic poem, as well as 23 prose homilies and a prose life of St. Guthlac, the *Vercelli Guthlac.* The book is so named because it was found in the cathedral library at Vercelli, northwestern Italy, in 1822. Marginalia in the manuscript indicate that the manuscript was in English use in the 11th century. It was probably taken to Italy by one of the numerous Anglo-Saxon pilgrims on the way to Rome.

CHAPTER 2

THE MIDDLE ENGLISH PERIOD

By the end of the Old English period, English had been established as a literary language with a polish and versatility unequaled among European vernaculars. The Norman Conquest (1066) worked no immediate transformation on either the language or the literature of the English.

EARLY MIDDLE ENGLISH POETRY

Older poetry continued to be copied during the last half of the 11th century. Two poems of the early 12th century— "Durham", which praises that city's cathedral and its relics, and *Instructions for Christians*, a didactic piece—show that correct alliterative verse could be composed well after 1066. But even before the conquest, rhyme had begun to supplant, rather than supplement, alliteration in some poems, which continued to use the older four-stress line, although their rhythms varied from the set types used in classical Old English verse. A postconquest example is "The Grave," which contains several rhyming lines. A poem from *The Anglo-Saxon Chronicle* on the death of William the Conqueror, lamenting his cruelty and greed, has more rhyme than alliteration.

Influence of French Poetry

By the end of the 12th century, English poetry had been so heavily influenced by French models that such a work as the long epic *Brut* (*c.* 1200) by Lawamon, a Worcestershire priest, seems archaic for mixing alliterative lines with rhyming couplets while generally eschewing French vocabulary. The *Brut* draws mainly upon Wace's Anglo-Norman *Roman de Brut* (1155; based in turn upon Geoffrey of Monmouth's *Historia regum Britanniae* [History of the Kings of Britain]), but in Lawamon's hands the Arthurian story takes on a Germanic and heroic flavour largely missing in Wace. The *Brut* exists in two manuscripts, one written shortly after 1200 and the other some 50 years later. That the later version has been extensively modernized and somewhat abridged suggests the speed with which English language and literary tastes were changing in this period. *The Proverbs of Alfred* was written somewhat earlier, in the late 12th century. These proverbs deliver conventional wisdom in a mixture of rhymed couplets and alliterative lines, and it is hardly likely that any of the material they contain actually originated with the king whose wisdom they celebrate. The early 13th-century *Bestiary* mixes alliterative lines, three- and four-stress couplets, and septenary (heptameter) lines, but the logic behind this mix is more obvious than in the *Brut* and the *Proverbs*, for the poet was imitating the varied metres of his Latin source. More regular in form than these poems is the anonymous *Poema morale* in septenary couplets, in which an old man delivers a dose of moral advice to his presumably younger audience.

By far the most brilliant poem of this period is *The Owl and the Nightingale* (written after 1189), an example of the popular debate genre. The two birds argue topics

Roman de Brut, *a chronicle of King Arthur (pictured encountering a giant roasting a pig), served as the basis for Lawamon's* Brut, *one of the few poems of its time not influenced by French verse.* British Library, London, UK/ The Bridgeman Art Library

ranging from their hygienic habits, looks, and songs to marriage, prognostication, and the proper modes of worship. The nightingale stands for the joyous aspects of life, the owl for the sombre. There is no clear winner, but the debate ends as the birds go off to state their cases to one Nicholas of Guildford, a wise man. The poem is learned in the clerical tradition but wears its learning lightly as the disputants speak in colloquial and sometimes earthy language. Like the *Poema morale*, *The Owl and the Nightingale* is metrically regular (octosyllabic couplets), but it uses the French metre with an assurance unusual in so early a poem.

Fabliau

The fabliau is a short metrical tale made popular in medieval France by the jongleurs, or professional storytellers. Fabliaux were characterized by vivid detail and realistic observation and were usually comic, coarse, and often cynical, especially in their treatment of women.

About 150 fabliaux are extant. Many of them are based on elementary jokes or puns—such as one called *Estula*, which can either be a person's name or mean "Are you there?"—or on wry situations, such as one tale in which a man is rescued from drowning but has his eye put out by the boat hook that saves him. The majority of fabliaux are erotic, and the merriment provoked often depends on situations and adventures that are sometimes obscene. Recurring characters include the cuckold and his wife, the lover, and the naughty priest. The theme of guile is often treated, frequently to show the deceiver deceived.

It was once widely held that fabliaux represented the literature of the bourgeois and common people. This, however, is unlikely, since they contain a substantial element of burlesque (or mockery and parody) that depends, for its appreciation, on considerable knowledge of courtly society, love, and manners. They also presuppose something like scorn for those of humble rank who ape their betters.

Some of the subject matter in the fabliaux can be paralleled in other times and other countries: many of the plots stem from folklore, some have classical affinities, and a few can be traced to Asian sources. But many of the tales are so simple that they could have arisen spontaneously. The earliest fabliau, *Richeut*, dates from approximately 1175, but the main period of fabliau composition was the 13th century, with an extension into the first half of the 14th. Most fabliaux are 200 to 400 lines in length, though there are extremes of fewer than 20 lines and of more than 1,300. Their authors included amateur writers (notably Philippe de Beaumanoir) and professionals (e.g., Jehan Bodel and Rutebeuf). Verse tales analogous to the fabliaux exist in other languages. Geoffrey Chaucer's "Reeve's Tale," for example, is based on a known fabliau, and several of the other comic tales in *The Canterbury Tales* may trace their origins to fabliaux.

DIDACTIC POETRY

The 13th century saw a rise in the popularity of long didactic poems presenting biblical narrative, saints' lives, or moral instruction for those untutored in Latin or French. The most idiosyncratic of these is the *Ormulum* by Orm, an Augustinian canon in the north of England. Written in some 20,000 lines arranged in unrhymed but metrically rigid couplets, the work is interesting mainly in that the manuscript that preserves it is Orm's autograph and shows his somewhat fussy efforts to reform and regularize English spelling. Other biblical paraphrases are *Genesis* and *Exodus, Jacob and Joseph*, and the vast *Cursor mundi*, whose subject, as its title suggests, is the history of the world. An especially popular work was the *South English Legendary*, which began as a miscellaneous collection of saints' lives but was expanded by later redactors and rearranged in the order of the church calendar. The didactic tradition continued into the 14th century with Robert Mannyng's *Handling Sin*, a confessional manual whose expected dryness is relieved by the insertion of lively narratives, and the *Prick of Conscience*, a popular summary of theology sometimes attributed to the mystic Richard Rolle.

VERSE ROMANCE

The earliest examples of verse romance, a genre that would remain popular through the Middle Ages, appeared in the 13th century. *King Horn* and *Floris and Blauncheflour* both are preserved in a manuscript of about 1250. *King Horn*, oddly written in short two- and three-stress lines, is a vigorous tale of a kingdom lost and regained, with a subplot concerning Horn's love for Princess Rymenhild. *Floris and Blauncheflour* is more exotic, being the tale of a pair of royal lovers who become separated and, after various adventures in eastern lands, reunited. Not much later than these is *The Lay of Havelok the Dane*, a tale of princely love and adventure similar to *King Horn* but more competently executed.

Many more such romances were produced in the 14th century. Popular subgenres were "the matter of Britain" (Arthurian romances such as *Of Arthour and of Merlin* and *Ywain and Gawain*), "the matter of Troy" (tales of antiquity such as *The Siege of Troy* and *King Alisaunder*), and the English Breton lays (stories of otherworldly magic, such as *Lai le Freine* and *Sir Orfeo*, modeled after those of professional Breton storytellers). These relatively unsophisticated works were written for a bourgeois audience, and the

Beast Epic

The beast epic is a popular genre in various literatures, consisting of a lengthy cycle of animal tales that provides a satiric commentary on human society. Although individual episodes may be drawn from fables, the beast epic differs from the fable not only in length but also in putting less emphasis on a moral.

The earliest European beast epics were in Latin, but vernacular epics in French, German, and Dutch existed in the late Middle Ages. Among the most famous are the 10th- and 11th-century cycles in which the hero is Reynard the Fox. The cycle includes the tale of the Fox and Chanticleer the Cock, the basis later of "The Nun's Priest's Tale" in Geoffrey Chaucer's *The Canterbury Tales*. John Dryden used the beast epic as the framework of the poem *The Hind and the Panther* (1687), and Joel Chandler Harris's *Uncle Remus: His Songs and His Sayings* (1880) derived many episodes from beast tales carried to the United States by African slaves. *Animal Farm* (1945), an antiutopian satire by George Orwell, is a modern adaptation of the beast tale.

manuscripts that preserve them are early examples of commercial book production.

The humorous beast epic makes its first appearance in Britain in the 13th century with *The Fox and the Wolf,* taken indirectly from the Old French *Roman de Renart.* In the same manuscript with this work is *Dame Sirith*, the earliest English fabliau. Another sort of humour is found in *The Land of Cockaygne*, which depicts a utopia better than heaven, where rivers run with milk, honey, and wine, geese fly about already roasted, and monks hunt with hawks and dance with nuns.

ARTHURIAN LEGEND

The term *Arthurian legend* describes the body of stories and medieval romances (also known as the matter of Britain, as indicated above) centring on the legendary king Arthur. Medieval writers, especially the French, variously treated stories of Arthur's birth, the adventures of his knights, and the adulterous love between his knight Sir Lancelot and his queen, Guinevere. This last situation and the quest for the Holy Grail (the vessel used by Christ at the Last Supper and given to Joseph of Arimathea) brought about the dissolution of the knightly fellowship, the death of Arthur, and the destruction of his kingdom.

Stories about Arthur and his court had been popular in Wales before the 11th century. European fame came through Geoffrey of Monmouth's *History of the Kings of Britain* (1135–38), celebrating a glorious and triumphant king who defeated a Roman army in eastern France but was mortally wounded in battle during a rebellion at home led by his nephew Mordred. Some features of Geoffrey's story were marvelous fabrications, and certain features of the Celtic stories were adapted to suit feudal times. The concept of Arthur as a world conqueror was clearly

Sir Bedivere returning Excalibur, Arthur's sword, to the lake from which it came. Illustration by Aubrey Beardsley for an edition of Sir Thomas Malory's *Le Morte Darthur*. Photos.com/Jupiterimages

inspired by legends surrounding great leaders such as Alexander the Great and Charlemagne. Later writers, notably Wace of Jersey and Lawamon, filled out certain details, especially in connection with Arthur's knightly fellowship (the Knights of the Round Table).

Using Celtic sources, the French poet Chrétien de Troyes in the late 12th century made Arthur the ruler of a realm of marvels in five romances of adventure. He also introduced the themes of the Grail and the love of Lancelot and Guinevere into Arthurian legend. Prose romances of the 13th century explored these major themes further. An early prose romance centring on Lancelot seems to have become the kernel of a cyclic work known as the Prose *Lancelot,* or Vulgate cycle (*c.* 1225).

The Lancelot theme was connected with the Grail story through Lancelot's son, the pure knight Sir Galahad, who achieved the vision of God through the Grail as fully as is possible in this life, whereas Sir Lancelot was impeded in his progress along the mystic way because of his adultery with Guinevere. Another branch of the Vulgate cycle was based on a very early 13th-century verse romance, the *Merlin*, by the French poet Robert de Boron, that had told of Arthur's birth and childhood and his winning of the crown by drawing a magic sword from a stone. The writer of the Vulgate cycle turned this into prose, adding a pseudo-historical narrative dealing with Arthur's military exploits. A final branch of the Vulgate cycle contained an account of Arthur's Roman campaign and war with Mordred, to which was added a story of Lancelot's renewed adultery with Guinevere and the disastrous war between Lancelot and Sir Gawain that ensued. A later prose romance, known as the post-Vulgate Grail romance (*c.* 1240), combined Arthurian legend with material from the Tristan romance.

The legend told in the Vulgate cycle and post-Vulgate romance was transmitted to English-speaking readers in Thomas Malory's late 15th-century prose *Le Morte Darthur*. At the same time, there was renewed interest in Geoffrey of Monmouth's *Historia*, and the fictitious kings of Britain became more or less incorporated with official national mythology. The legend remained alive during the 17th century, though interest in it was by then confined to England. Of merely antiquarian interest during the 18th century, it again figured in literature during Victorian times, notably in Alfred Tennyson's *Idylls of the King*, and in the 20th century it inspired a wide variety of poems, novels, and films.

Breton Lay

The Breton lay (Middle English: *lai breton*) is a poetic form so called because Breton professional storytellers supposedly recited similar poems, though none are extant. A short, rhymed romance recounting a love story, it includes supernatural elements, mythology transformed by medieval chivalry, and the Celtic idea of faerie, the land of enchantment. Derived from the late 12th-century French lais of Marie de France, it was adapted into English in the late 13th century and became very popular. The few extant English Breton lays include *Sir Gowther* (c. 1400), a version of the story of Robert the Devil; the incomplete, early 14th-century *Lai le Freine*; *Sir Orfeo*, a recasting of the Orpheus and Eurydice story; the 14th-century *Sir Launfal*, or *Launfalus Miles*, an Arthurian romance by Thomas Chestre; *Sir Emare*, of the late 14th or early 15th century, on the theme of the constant wife; and the 15th-century Sir Landeval, a variant of *Sir Launfal*. Some of Geoffrey Chaucer's *Canterbury Tales* are derived from Breton lays.

THE LYRIC

The lyric was virtually unknown to Old English poets. Poems such as "Deor" and "Wulf and Eadwacer," which have been called lyrics, are thematically different from those that began to circulate orally in the 12th century and to be written down in great numbers in the 13th century.

These Old English poems also have a stronger narrative component than the later productions. The most frequent topics in the Middle English secular lyric are springtime and romantic love. Many rework such themes tediously, but some, such as *"Foweles in the Frith"* (13th century) and "Ich am of Irlaunde" (14th century), convey strong emotions in a few lines. Two lyrics of the early 13th century, "Mirie it is while sumer ilast" and "Sumer is icumen in," are preserved with musical settings, and probably most of the others were meant to be sung.

The dominant mood of the religious lyrics is passionate: the poets sorrow for Christ on the cross and for the Virgin Mary, celebrate the "five joys" of Mary, and import language from love poetry to express religious devotion. Excellent early examples are "Nou goth sonne under wod" and "Stond wel, moder, ounder rode". Many of the lyrics are preserved in manuscript anthologies, of which the best is British Library manuscript Harley 2253 from the early 14th century. In this collection, known as the *Harley Lyrics*, the love poems, such as "Alysoun" and "Blow, Northern Wind," take after the poems of the Provençal troubadours but are less formal, less abstract, and more lively. The religious lyrics also are of high quality. But the most remarkable of the Harley Lyrics, "The Man in the Moon," far from being about love or religion, imagines the man in the Moon as a simple peasant, sympathizes with his hard life, and offers him some useful advice on how to best the village hayward (a local officer in charge of a town's common herd of cattle).

A poem such as "The Man in the Moon" serves as a reminder that, although the poetry of the early Middle English period was increasingly influenced by the Anglo-Norman literature produced for the courts, it is seldom "courtly." Most English poets, whether writing about kings or peasants, looked at life from a bourgeois perspective. If their work sometimes lacks sophistication, it nevertheless has a vitality that comes from preoccupation with daily affairs.

EARLY MIDDLE ENGLISH PROSE

Old English prose texts were copied for more than a century after the Norman Conquest. The homilies of Aelfric were especially popular, and King Alfred's translations of Boethius and Augustine survive only in 12th-century manuscripts. In the early 13th century an anonymous worker at Worcester supplied glosses to certain words in a number of Old English manuscripts, which demonstrates that by this time the older language was beginning to pose difficulties for readers.

The composition of English prose also continued without interruption. Two manuscripts of *The Anglo-Saxon Chronicle* exhibit very strong prose for years after the conquest, and one of these, the Peterborough Chronicle, continues to 1154. Two manuscripts of about 1200 contain 12th-century sermons, and another has the workmanlike compilation *Vices and Virtues*, composed about 1200. But the English language faced stiff competition from both Anglo-Norman (the insular dialect of French being used increasingly in the monasteries) and Latin, a language intelligible to speakers of both English and French.

It was inevitable, then, that the production of English prose should decline in quantity, if not in quality. The great prose works of this period were composed mainly for those who could read only English—women especially. In the West Midlands the Old English alliterative prose tradition remained very much alive into the 13th century, when the several texts known collectively as the *Katherine*

Group were written. *St. Katherine*, *St. Margaret*, and *St. Juliana*, found together in a single manuscript, have rhythms strongly reminiscent of those of Aelfric and Wulfstan. So to a lesser extent do *Hali Meithhad* ("Holy Maidenhood") and *Sawles Warde* ("The Guardianship of the Soul") from the same book, but newer influences can be seen in these works as well: as the title of another devotional piece, *The Wohunge of Ure Lauerd* ("The Wooing of Our Lord"), suggests, the prose of this time often has a rapturous, even sensual flavour, and, like the poetry, it frequently employs the language of love to express religious fervour.

Further removed from the Old English prose tradition, though often associated with the *Katherine Group*, is the *Ancrene Wisse* ("Guide for Anchoresses," also known as the *Ancrene Riwle,* or "Rule for Anchoresses"), a manual for the guidance of women recluses outside the regular orders. This anonymous work, which was translated into French and Latin and remained popular until the 16th century, is notable for its humanity, practicality, and insight into human nature but even more for its brilliant style. Like the other prose of its time, it uses alliteration as ornament, but it is more indebted to new fashions in preaching, which had originated in the universities, than to native traditions. With its richly figurative language, rhetorically crafted sentences, and carefully logical divisions and subdivisions, it manages to achieve in English the effects that such contemporary writers as John of Salisbury and Walter Map were striving for in Latin.

Little noteworthy prose was written in the late 13th century. In the early 14th century Dan Michel of Northgate produced in Kentish the *Ayenbite of Inwit* (*Prick of Conscience*), a translation from French. But the best prose of this time is by the mystic Richard Rolle, the hermit of Hampole, whose English tracts include *The Commandment,*

Meditations on the Passion, and *The Form of Perfect Living,* among others. His intense and stylized prose was among the most popular of the 14th century and inspired such later works as Walter Hilton's *Scale of Perfection,* Julian of Norwich's *Sixteen Revelations of Divine Love,* and the anonymous *Cloud of Unknowing.*

LATER MIDDLE ENGLISH POETRY

The most puzzling episode in the development of later Middle English literature is the apparently sudden reappearance of unrhymed alliterative poetry in the mid-14th century. Debate continues as to whether the group of long, serious, and sometimes learned poems written between about 1350 and the first decade of the 15th century should be regarded as an "alliterative revival" or, rather, as the late flowering of a largely lost native tradition stretching back to the Old English period.

ALLITERATIVE POETRY

The earliest examples of the alliteration phenomenon, *William of Palerne* and *Winner and Waster,* are both datable to the 1350s, but neither poem exhibits to the full all the characteristics of the slightly later poems central to the movement. *William of Palerne,* condescendingly commissioned by a nobleman for the benefit of "them that know no French," is a homely paraphrase of a courtly Continental romance, the only poem in the group to take love as its central theme. The poet's technical competence in handling the difficult syntax and diction of the alliterative style is not, however, to be compared with that of *Winner and Waster*'s author, who exhibits full mastery of the form, particularly in descriptions of setting and spectacle. This poem's topical concern with social satire links it primarily with another, less formal body of alliterative verse, of which William Langland's *Piers Plowman* was the principal representative and exemplar. Indeed, *Winner and Waster,* with its sense of social commitment and occasional apocalyptic gesture, may well have served as a source of inspiration for Langland himself.

The term *alliterative revival* should not be taken to imply a return to the principles of classical Old English versification. The authors of the later 14th-century alliterative poems either inherited or developed their own conventions, which resemble those of the Old English tradition in only the most general way. The syntax and particularly the diction of later Middle English alliterative verse were also distinctive, and the search for alliterating phrases and constructions led to the extensive use of archaic, technical, and dialectal words. Hunts, feasts, battles, storms, and landscapes were described with a brilliant concretion of detail rarely paralleled since, while the abler poets also contrived subtle modulations of the staple verse-paragraph to accommodate dialogue, discourse, and argument.

Among the poems central to the movement were three pieces dealing with the life and legends of Alexander the Great, the massive Destruction of Troy, and the Siege of Jerusalem. The fact that all of these derived from various Latin sources suggests that the anonymous poets were likely to have been clerics with a strong, if bookish, historical sense of their romance "matters." The "matter of Britain" was represented by an outstanding composition, the alliterative *Morte Arthure*, an epic portrayal of King Arthur's conquests in Europe and his eventual fall, which combined a strong narrative thrust with considerable density and subtlety of diction. A gathering sense of inevitable transitoriness gradually tempers the virile realization of heroic idealism, and it is not surprising to find that the poem was later used by Sir Thomas Malory as a source for his prose account of the Arthurian legend, *Le Morte Darthur* (completed *c.* 1470).

The alliterative movement would today be regarded as a curious but inconsiderable episode were it not for four other poems now generally attributed to a single anonymous author: the chivalric romance *Sir Gawayne and the Grene Knight*, two homiletic poems called *Patience* and *Purity* (or *Cleanness*), and an elegiac dream vision known as

An illustration from Sir Gawayne and the Grene Knight, *which is considered a technical masterpiece and one of four poems that best exemplify 14th-century alliterative verse.* Hulton Archive/Getty Images

Pearl, all miraculously preserved in a single manuscript dated about 1400. The poet of *Sir Gawayne* far exceeded the other alliterative writers in his mastery of form and style, and, though he wrote ultimately as a moralist, human warmth and sympathy (often taking comic form) are also close to the heart of his work.

Patience relates the biblical story of Jonah as a human comedy of petulance and irascibility set off against God's benign forbearance. *Purity* imaginatively re-creates several monitory narratives of human impurity and its consequences in a spectacular display of poetic skill: the Flood, the destruction of Sodom, and Belshazzar's Feast. The poet's principal achievement, however, was *Sir Gawayne*, in which he used the conventional apparatus of chivalric romance to engage in a serious exploration of moral conduct in the face of the unknown. The hero, Gawain, a questing knight of Arthur's court, embodies a combination of the noblest chivalric and spiritual aspirations of the age, but, instead of triumphing in the conventional way, he fails when tested (albeit rather unfairly) by mysterious supernatural powers. No paraphrase can hope to recapture the imaginative resources displayed in the telling of the story and the structuring of the poem as a work of art.

Pearl stands somewhat aside from the alliterative movement proper. In common with a number of other poems of the period, it was composed in stanzaic form, with alliteration used for ornamental effect. Technically, it is one of the most complex poems in the language, an attempt to work in words an analogy to the jeweler's art. The jeweler-poet is vouchsafed a heavenly vision in which he sees his pearl, the discreet symbol used in the poem for a lost infant daughter who has died to become a bride of Christ. She offers theological consolation for his grief, expounding the way of salvation and the place of human life in a transcendental and extra-temporal view of things.

The alliterative movement was primarily confined to poets writing in northern and northwestern England, who showed little regard for courtly, London-based literary developments. It is likely that alliterative poetry, under aristocratic patronage, filled a gap in the literary life of the provinces caused by the decline of Anglo-Norman in the latter half of the 14th century. Alliterative poetry was not unknown in London and the southeast, but it penetrated those areas in a modified form and in poems that dealt with different subject matter.

William Langland's long alliterative poem *Piers Plowman* begins with a vision of the world seen from the Malvern Hills in Worcestershire, where, tradition has it, the poet was born and brought up and where he would have been open to the influence of the alliterative movement. If what he tells about himself in the poem is true (and there is no other source of information), he later lived obscurely in London as an unbeneficed cleric.

Langland wrote in the unrhymed alliterative mode, but he modified it in such a way as to make it more accessible to a wider audience by treating the metre more loosely and avoiding the arcane diction of the provincial poets. His poem exists in at least three and possibly four versions: A) *Piers Plowman* in its short early form, dating from the 1360s; B) a major revision and extension of A made in the late 1370s; C) (1380s), a less "literary" version of B, apparently intended to bring its doctrinal issues into clearer focus; and Z) a conjectured version that calls into question the dating for A, B, and C. The poem takes the form of a series of dream visions dealing with the social and spiritual predicament of late 14th-century England against a sombre apocalyptic backdrop. Realistic and allegorical elements are mingled in a phantasmagoric way, and both the poetic medium and the structure are frequently subverted by the writer's spiritual and didactic impulses. Passages of involuted theological reasoning mingle with scatological satire, and moments of sublime religious feeling appear alongside forthright political comment. This makes it a work of the utmost difficulty, defiant of categorization, but at the same time Langland never fails to convince the reader of the passionate integrity of his writing. His bitter attacks on political and ecclesiastical corruption (especially among the friars) quickly struck chords with his contemporaries. Among minor poems in the same vein are *Mum and the Sothsegger* (*c.* 1399–1406) and a Lollard piece called *Pierce the Ploughman's Creed* (*c.* 1395). In the 16th century, *Piers Plowman* was issued as a printed book and was used for apologetic purposes by the early Protestants.

COURTLY POETRY

Apart from a few late and minor reappearances in Scotland and the northwest of England, the alliterative movement was over before the first quarter of the 15th century had passed. The other major strand in the development of English poetry from roughly 1350 proved much more durable. The cultivation and refinement of human sentiment with respect to love, already present in earlier 14th-century writings such as the *Harley Lyrics*, took firm root in English court culture during the reign of Richard II (1377–99). English began to displace Anglo-Norman as the language spoken at court and in aristocratic circles, and signs of royal and noble patronage for English vernacular writers became evident. These processes undoubtedly created some of the conditions in which a writer of

Chaucer's interests and temperament might flourish, but they were encouraged and given direction by his genius in establishing English as a literary language.

The numerous 15th-century followers of Chaucer continued to treat the conventional range of courtly and moralizing topics, but only rarely with the intelligence and stylistic accomplishment of their distinguished predecessors. The canon of Chaucer's works began to accumulate delightful but apocryphal trifles such as *The Flower and the Leaf* and *The Assembly of Ladies* (both *c.* 1475), the former, like a surprising quantity of 15th-century verse of this type, purportedly written by a woman. The stock figures of the ardent but endlessly frustrated lover and the irresistible but disdainful lady were cultivated as part of the "game of love" depicted in numerous courtly lyrics. By the 15th century, vernacular literacy was spreading rapidly among both men and women of the laity, with the influence of French courtly love poetry remaining strong. Aristocratic and knightly versifiers such as Charles, duc d'Orléans (captured at Agincourt in 1415), his "jailer" William de la Pole, duke of Suffolk, and Sir Richard Ros (translator of Alain Chartier's influential *La Belle Dame sans merci*) were widely read and imitated among the gentry and in bourgeois circles well into the 16th century.

Both Chaucer and his friend John Gower—Chaucer's contemporary, who provides a contrast to Chaucer in that the sober and earnest moral intent behind Gower's writing is always clear, whereas Chaucer can be noncommittal and evasive—had to some extent enjoyed royal and aristocratic patronage, and the active seeking of patronage became a pervasive feature of the 15th-century literary scene. Thomas Hoccleve, a minor civil servant who probably knew Chaucer and claimed to be his disciple, dedicated *The Regiment of Princes* (*c.* 1412), culled from an

earlier work of the same name, to the future king Henry V.
Most of Hoccleve's compositions seem to have been written with an eye to patronage, and, though they occasionally
yield unexpected glimpses of his daily and private lives,
they have little to recommend them as poetry. Hoccleve's
aspiration to be Chaucer's successor was rapidly overshad-
owed, in sheer bulk if not necessarily in literary merit, by
the formidable oeuvre of John Lydgate, a monk at the
abbey of Bury St. Edmunds.

Lydgate, too, was greatly stimulated at the prospects
opened up by distinguished patronage and produced as a
result a number of very long pieces that were greatly
admired in their day. A staunch Lancastrian, Lydgate dedicated his *Troy Book* (1412–21) and *Life of Our Lady* to Henry
V and his *Fall of Princes* (1431–38; based ultimately on
Boccaccio's *De casibus virorum illustrium*) to Humphrey
Plantagenet, duke of Gloucester. He also essayed courtly
verse in Chaucer's manner (*The Complaint of the Black
Knight* and *The Temple of Glass*), but his imitation of the
master's style was rarely successful. Both Lydgate and
Hoccleve admired above all Chaucer's "eloquence," by
which they meant mainly the Latinate elements in his diction. Their own painfully polysyllabic style, which came to
be known as the "aureate" style, was widely imitated for
more than a century. In sum, the major 15th-century
English poets were generally undistinguished as successors of Chaucer, and, for a significant but independent
extension of his achievement, one must look to the
Scottish courtly poets known as the *makaris* ("makers"),
among whom were King James I of Scotland, Robert
Henryson, and William Dunbar.

Lydgate's following at court gave him a central place in
15th-century literary life, but the typical concerns shown
by his verse do not distinguish it from a great body of religious, moral, historical, and didactic writing, much of it

Prolific 14th-century court poet John Lydgate wrote largely with an eye toward patronage. While widely admired and read during his lifetime and for more than a century afterward, Lydgate's vast output is today largely ignored. Archive Photos/Getty Images

anonymous. A few identifiable provincial writers turn out to have had their own local patrons, often among the country gentry. East Anglia may be said to have produced a minor school in the works of John Capgrave, Osbern Bokenam, and John Metham, among others also active during the middle of the century. Some of the most moving and accomplished verse of the time is to be found in the anonymous lyrics and carols (songs with a refrain) on conventional subjects such as the transience of life, the coming of death, the sufferings of Christ, and other penitential themes. The author of some distinctive poems in this mode was John Audelay of Shropshire, whose style was heavily influenced by the alliterative movement. Literary devotion to the Virgin Mary was particularly prominent and at its best could produce masterpieces of artful simplicity, such as the poem "I sing of a maiden that is makeless" [matchless].

POPULAR AND SECULAR VERSE

The art that conceals art was also characteristic of the best popular and secular verse of the period, outside the courtly mode. Some of the shorter verse romances, usually in a form called tail rhyme, were far from negligible: *Ywain and Gawain*, from the *Yvain* of Chrétien de Troyes; *Sir Launfal*, after Marie de France's *Lanval*; and *Sir Degrevant*. Humorous and lewd songs, versified tales, folk songs, ballads, and others form a lively body of compositions. Oral transmission was probably common, and the survival of much of what is extant is fortuitous. The manuscript known as the Percy Folio, a 17th-century antiquarian collection of such material, may be a fair sampling of the repertoire of the late medieval itinerant entertainer. In addition to a number of popular romances of the type satirized long before by Chaucer in *Sir Thopas*, the Percy manuscript also contains a number of impressive ballads very much like those collected from oral sources in the 18th and 19th centuries. The extent of medieval origin of the poems collected in Francis J. Child's *English and Scottish Popular Ballads* (1882–98) is debatable. Several of the Robin Hood ballads undoubtedly were known in the 15th century, and the characteristic laconically repetitious and incremental style of the ballads is also to be seen in the enigmatic "Corpus Christi Carol," preserved in an early 16th-century London grocer's commonplace book. In the same manuscript, but in a rather different vein, is *The Nut-Brown Maid*, an expertly managed dialogue-poem on female constancy.

Political Verse

A genre that does not fit easily into the categories already mentioned is political verse, of which a good deal was written in the 15th century. Much of it was avowedly and often crudely propagandist, especially during the Wars of the Roses, though a piece like the *Agincourt Carol* shows that it was already possible to strike the characteristically English note of insular patriotism soon after 1415. Of particular interest is the *Libel of English Policy* (c. 1436) on another typically English theme of a related kind: "Cherish merchandise, keep the admiralty, / That we be masters of the narrow sea."

LATER MIDDLE ENGLISH PROSE

The continuity of a tradition in English prose writing, linking the later with the early Middle English period, is somewhat clearer than that detected in verse. The *Ancrene Wisse*, for example, continued to be copied and adapted to suit changing tastes and circumstances. But sudden and brilliant imaginative phenomena like the writings of Chaucer, Langland, and the author of *Sir Gawayne* are not to be found in prose. Instead came steady growth in the composition of religious prose of various kinds and the first appearance of secular prose in any quantity.

RELIGIOUS PROSE

Of the first importance was the development of a sober, analytical, but nonetheless impressive kind of contemplative or mystical prose, represented by Walter Hilton's *Scale of Perfection* and the anonymous *Cloud of Unknowing*. The authors of these pieces certainly knew the more rugged and fervent writings of their earlier, 14th-century predecessor Richard Rolle, and to some extent they reacted against what they saw as excesses in the style and content of his work. It is of particular interest to note that the mystical tradition was continued into the 15th century, though in very different ways, by two women writers, Julian of Norwich and Margery Kempe. Julian, often regarded as the first English woman of letters, underwent a series of mystical experiences in 1373 about which she wrote in her *Sixteen Revelations of Divine Love*, one of the foremost works of English spirituality by the standards of any age. Rather different religious experiences went into the making of *The Book of Margery Kempe* (*c.* 1432–36), the extraordinary autobiographical record of a bourgeoise woman, dictated to two clerks. The nature and status of its spiritual content remain controversial, but its often engaging colloquial style and vivid realization of the medieval scene are of abiding interest.

Another important branch of the contemplative movement in prose involved the translation of Continental Latin texts. A major example, and one of the best-loved of all medieval English books in its time, is *The Mirror of the Blessed Life of Jesus Christ* (*c.* 1410), Nicholas Love's translation of the *Meditationes vitae Christi*, attributed to St. Bonaventure. Love's work was particularly valued by the church as an orthodox counterbalance to the heretical tendencies of the Lollards, who espoused the teachings of

John Wycliffe and his circle. The Lollard movement generated a good deal of stylistically distinctive prose writing,
though as the Lollards soon came under threat of death by
burning, nearly all of it remains anonymous. A number of
English works have been attributed to Wycliffe himself,
and the first English translation of the Bible to Wycliffe's
disciple John Purvey, but there are no firm grounds for
these attributions. The Lollard Bible, which exists in a
crude early form and in a more impressive later version
(supposedly Purvey's work), was widely read in spite of
being under doctrinal suspicion. It later influenced
William Tyndale's translation of the New Testament, completed in 1525, and, through Tyndale, the King James
Version (1611).

SECULAR PROSE

Secular compositions and translations in prose also came
into prominence in the last quarter of the 14th century,
though their stylistic accomplishment does not always
match that of the religious tradition. Chaucer's *Tale of
Melibeus* and his two astronomical translations, the *Treatise
on the Astrolabe* and the *Equatorie of the Planets*, were relatively modest endeavours beside the massive efforts of
John of Trevisa, who translated from Latin both Ranulf
Higden's *Polychronicon* (c. 1385–87), a universal history, and
Bartholomaeus Anglicus's *De proprietatibus rerum* (1398;
"On the Properties of Things"), an encyclopaedia. Judging
by the number of surviving manuscripts, however, the
most widely read secular prose work of the period is likely
to have been *The Voyage and Travels of Sir John Mandeville*,
the supposed adventures of Sir John Mandeville, knight of
St. Albans, on his journeys through Asia. Though the work
now is believed to be purely fictional, its exotic allure and

the occasionally arch style of its author were popular with the English reading public down to the 18th century.

The 15th century saw the consolidation of English prose as a respectable medium for serious writings of various kinds. The anonymous *Brut* chronicle survives in more manuscripts than any other medieval English work and was instrumental in fostering a new sense of national identity. John Capgrave's *Chronicle of England* (*c.* 1462) and Sir John Fortescue's *On the Governance of England* (*c.* 1470) were part of the same trend. At its best, the style of such works could be vigorous and straightforward, close to the language of everyday speech, like that found in the chance survivals of private letters of the period. Best known and most numerous among letters are those of the Paston family of Norfolk, but significant collections were also left by the Celys of London and the Stonors of Oxfordshire. More-eccentric prose stylists of the period were the religious controversialist Reginald Pecock and John Skelton, whose aureate translation of the *Bibliotheca historica* of Diodorus Siculus stands in marked contrast to the demotic exuberance of his verse.

The crowning achievement of later Middle English prose writing was Sir Thomas Malory's cycle of Arthurian legends, which was given the title *Le Morte Darthur* by William Caxton when he printed his edition in 1485. There is still uncertainty as to the identity of Malory, who described himself as a "knight-prisoner." The characteristic mixture of chivalric nostalgia and tragic feeling with which he imbued his book gave fresh inspiration to the tradition of writing on Arthurian themes. The nature of Malory's artistry eludes easy definition, and the degree to which the effects he achieved were a matter of conscious contrivance on his part is debatable. Much of *Le Morte Darthur* was translated from prolix French prose romances, and Malory evidently selected and condensed his material with instinctive mastery as he went along. At the same time, he cast narrative and dialogue in the cadences of a virile and natural English prose that matched the nobility of both the characters and the theme.

MIDDLE ENGLISH DRAMA

Because the manuscripts of medieval English plays were usually ephemeral performance scripts rather than reading matter, very few examples have survived from what once must have been a very large dramatic literature. What little survives from before the 15th century includes some bilingual fragments, indicating that the same play might have been given in English or Anglo-Norman, according to the composition of the audience. From the late 14th century onward, three main dramatic genres are discernible: the mystery, or Corpus Christi, cycles, the morality plays, and the miracle plays.

MYSTERY PLAYS

The mystery plays were long cyclic dramas of the Creation, Fall, and Redemption of humankind, based mostly on biblical narratives. They usually included a selection of Old Testament episodes (such as the stories of Cain and Abel and of Abraham and Isaac) but concentrated mainly on the life and Passion of Jesus Christ. They always ended with the Last Judgment. The cycles were generally financed and performed by the craft guilds and staged on wagons in the streets and squares of the towns. Texts of the cycles staged at York, Chester, and Wakefield and at an unstated location in East Anglia (the so-called N-Town plays) have survived, together with fragments from Coventry,

Newcastle, and Norwich. Their literary quality is uneven, but the York cycle (probably the oldest) has an impressively realized version of Christ's Passion by a dramatist influenced by the alliterative style in verse. The Wakefield cycle has several particularly brilliant plays, attributed to the anonymous Wakefield Master, and his *the castle* is one of the masterpieces of medieval English literature.

YORK PLAYS

The York plays, a cycle of 48 plays dating from the 14th century, were performed during the Middle Ages by craft guilds in the city of York, in the north of England, on the summer feast day of Corpus Christi. They are of unknown authorship. Some of the York plays are almost identical with corresponding plays in the Wakefield cycle, and it has been suggested that there was an original (now lost) from which both cycles descended. It is more likely, however, that the York cycle was transferred bodily to Wakefield some time during the later 14th century and there established as a Corpus Christi cycle.

The plays were given in York on one day, in chronological order, on pageant wagons proceeding from one selected place to another. The cycle covers the story of man's fall and redemption, from the creation of the angels to the Last Judgment. Six plays are peculiar to York: Herod's son, the Transfiguration, Pilate's wife, Pilate's majordomo, the high priests' purchase of the field of blood, and of the appearance of the Virgin to the Apostle Thomas.

In the last revision of the York plays, about 14 plays (mainly those concerning Christ's Passion) were redacted into alliterative verse. These are powerful and the work of a dramatic genius, often referred to as the York Realist.

The York plays have been preserved in the Ashburnham Manuscript, in the British Library.

CHESTER PLAYS

The Chester plays, a 14th-century cycle of 25 scriptural plays, were performed at the prosperous city of Chester, in northern England, during the Middle Ages. They are traditionally dated about 1325, but a date of about 1375 has also been suggested. They were presented on three successive days at Corpus Christi, a religious feast day that falls in summer. On the first day there was a performance of plays 1–9 (including the fall of Lucifer, key episodes in the Old Testament, the Nativity, and the adoration of the Wise Men); on the second day a performance of plays 10–18 (including the flight into Egypt, Jesus' ministry, the Passion and Crucifixion, the Descent into Hell, and the arrival in paradise of the virtuous who had died before the Redemption had been achieved); and, finally, on the third day a performance of plays 19–25 (including the Resurrection, the Ascension of Christ into heaven, the Descent of the Holy Spirit, the coming of the Antichrist, and the Last Judgment).

The Chester plays are rich in content, yet tell the great story of human redemption more simply than the other surviving cycles. The text, containing more than 11,000 lines of verse, has been preserved in five manuscripts, which are kept in the Bodleian Library, Oxford, Eng.; the Huntington Library, San Marino, Calif., U.S.; and the British Museum, London.

WAKEFIELD PLAYS

The Wakefield plays, a cycle of 32 scriptural plays of the early 15th century, were performed during the Middle Ages at Wakefield, a town in the north of England, as part of the summertime religious festival of Corpus Christi. The text of the plays has been preserved in the Towneley

Manuscript (so called after a family that once owned it), now in the Huntington Library in California; the name of the manuscript has been extended to the plays themselves, which are sometimes called called the Towneley plays.

At some time, probably in the later 14th century, the plays performed at York were most likely transferred bodily to Wakefield and there established as a Corpus Christi cycle; six of the plays in each are virtually identical, and there are corresponding speeches here and there in others. On the whole, however, each cycle went its own way after the transfer. From a purely literary point of view, the Wakefield plays are considered superior to any other surviving cycle. In particular, the work of a talented reviser, known as the Wakefield Master, is easily recognizable for its brilliant handling of metre, language, and rhyme, and for its wit and satire. His *Second Shepherds' Play* is widely considered the greatest work of medieval English drama.

It is not known how long the cycle, which begins with the fall of Lucifer and ends with the Last Judgment, took in performance. The Chester cycle, which is shorter, was given over three days. The York cycle, which is longer, was given in one. Two plays (about Jacob) are peculiar to the Wakefield cycle, which omits many narratives from the New Testament that are found in all the other surviving cycles.

N-Town Plays

The N-Town plays, an English cycle of 42 scriptural plays dating from the second half of the 15th century, are so called because an opening proclamation refers to performance "in N. town." Since evidence suggests that the cycle was not peculiar to one city or community but traveled from town to town, the abbreviation "N." would indicate that the appropriate name of the town at which the cycle was being presented would have been inserted by the speaker.

The cycle is preserved in the Hegge Manuscript, so called after its 17th-century owner, Sir Robert Hegge, and it is therefore sometimes referred to as the Hegge cycle. On the flyleaf of the Hegge Manuscript is written "Ludus Conventriae" ("Play of Coventry"), and until the 19th century it was believed that the plays represented the Coventry cycle, until individual plays from Coventry were discovered and found to be totally different from equivalent plays in the N-Town cycle. Some scholars have attempted to show that the N-Town cycle is closely related to the (lost) cycle that was performed at Lincoln.

The N-Town cycle begins with the creation of the angels and the Fall of Lucifer and ends with the Assumption of the Virgin and the Last Judgment. Among the plays with no equivalent in other cycles are one on the death of Cain and five whose central figure is that of the Virgin, with whom the cycle is generally much preoccupied. Typically the N-Town plays are grave and dignified. The comic relief distinguishing other surviving cycles (from Chester, York, Wakefield) is markedly absent. A basic difference between the N-Town plays and those of the other cycles is that this cycle, because it was a traveling one, was apparently presented by professional actors. It did not use pageant wagons, whereby plays were presented as a procession, but was given in a single open space, with "mansions" (indicating general scenes) set up about a single acting area. The performances may have taken place over two successive days.

MORALITY PLAYS

The morality plays were allegorical dramas depicting the progress of a single character, representing the whole of humankind, from the cradle to the grave and sometimes beyond. The other dramatis personae might include God and the Devil but usually consisted of personified abstractions, such as the Vices and Virtues, Death, Penance, Mercy, and so forth. A varied collection of the moralities is known as the Macro Plays (*The Castle of Perseverance, Wisdom, Mankind*), but the single most impressive piece is *Everyman*, an English rendering of a Dutch play on the subject of the coming of death. Both the mystery and morality plays were frequently revived and performed into the 21st century.

The action of the morality play centres on a hero, such as Mankind, whose inherent weaknesses are assaulted by such personified diabolic forces as the Seven Deadly Sins but who may choose redemption and enlist the aid of such figures as the Four Daughters of God (Mercy, Justice, Temperance, and Truth).

Morality plays were an intermediate step in the transition from liturgical to professional secular drama and combine elements of each. They were performed by quasi-professional groups of actors who relied on public support. Thus the plays were usually short, their serious themes tempered by elements of farce. In the Dutch play *Het esbatement den appelboom* ("The Miraculous Apple Tree"), for example, a pious couple, Staunch Goodfellow and Steadfast Faith, are rewarded when God creates for them an everbearing apple tree with the property that whoever touches it without permission becomes stuck fast. This leads to predictable and humorous consequences.

The most famous of the French morality plays is Nicolas de la Chesnaye's *Condemnation des banquets* (1507), which argues for moderation by showing the bad end that awaits a company of unrepentant revelers, including Gluttony and Watering Mouth. Among the oldest of morality plays surviving in English is *The Castle of Perseverance* (c.

1425), about the battle for the soul of Humanum Genus. A plan for the staging of one performance has survived that depicts an outdoor theatre-in-the-round with the castle of the title at the centre.

Everyman

Of all morality plays, the one that is considered the greatest, and that is still performed, is *Everyman*. Written during the 15th century, it is probably a version of a Dutch play, *Elckerlyc*. It achieves a beautiful, simple solemnity in treating allegorically the theme of death and the fate of the human soul—of Everyman's soul as he tries to justify his time on earth. Though morality plays on the whole failed to achieve the vigorous realism of the Middle Ages' scriptural drama, this short play (about 900 lines) is more than an allegorical sermon, because vivid characterization gives it dramatic energy.

MIRACLE PLAYS

The miracle play is the third of the three principal kinds of vernacular drama of the European Middle Ages. It presents a real or fictitious account of the life, miracles, or martyrdom of a saint. The genre evolved from liturgical offices developed during the 10th and 11th centuries to enhance calendar festivals. By the 13th century they had become vernacularized and filled with unecclesiastical elements. They had been divorced from church services and were performed at public festivals. Almost all surviving miracle plays concern either the Virgin Mary or St. Nicholas, the 4th-century bishop of Myra in Asia Minor. Both Mary and Nicholas had active cults during the Middle Ages, and belief in the healing powers of saintly relics was widespread. In this climate, miracle plays flourished.

The Mary plays consistently involve her in the role of deus ex machina, coming to the aid of all who invoke her, be they worthy or wanton. She saves, for example, a priest who has sold his soul to the devil, a woman falsely accused of murdering her own child, and a pregnant abbess. Typical of these is a play called *St. John the Hairy*. At the outset the title character seduces and murders a princess. Upon capture, he is proclaimed a saint by an infant. He confesses his crime, whereupon God and Mary appear and aid John in reviving the princess, which done, the murderer saint is made a bishop.

The Nicholas plays are similar, an example being Jean Bodel's *Le Jeu de Saint Nicolas* (*c.* 1200), which details the deliverance of a crusader and the conversion of a Saracen king. Few English miracle plays are extant, because they were banned by Henry VIII in the mid-16th century and most were subsequently destroyed or lost.

THE TRANSITION FROM MEDIEVAL TO RENAISSANCE

The 15th century was a major period of growth in lay literacy, a process powerfully expedited by the introduction into England of printing by William Caxton in 1476. Caxton published Malory's *Le Morte Darthur* in the same year (1485) that Henry Tudor acceded to the throne as Henry VII, and the period from this time to the mid-16th century has been called the transition from medieval to Renaissance in English literature. A typical figure was the translator Alexander Barclay. His *Eclogues* (*c.* 1515), drawn from 15th-century Italian humanist sources, was an early essay in the fashionable Renaissance genre of pastoral, while his rendering of Sebastian Brant's *Narrenschiff* as *The*

Ship of Fools (1509) is a thoroughly medieval satire on con-temporary folly and corruption. *The Pastime of Pleasure* (completed in 1506; published 1509) by Stephen Hawes, ostensibly an allegorical romance in Lydgate's manner, unexpectedly adumbrates the great Tudor theme of aca-demic cultivation as a necessary accomplishment of the courtly knight or gentleman.

The themes of education and good government pre-dominate in the new humanist writing of the 16th century, both in discursive prose (such as Sir Thomas Elyot's *The Book Named the Governor* [1531] and Roger Ascham's *Toxophilus* [1545; "Lover of the Bow"] and *The Schoolmaster* [1570]) and in drama (the plays of Henry Medwall and Richard Rastall). The preeminent work of English human-ism, Sir Thomas More's *Utopia* (1516), was composed in Latin and appeared in an English translation in 1551. The most distinctive voice in the poetry of the time was that of John Skelton, tutor to Henry VII's sons and author of an extraordinary range of writing, often in an equally extraor-dinary style. His works include a long play, *Magnificence* (1516), like his *Bowge of Court* (c. 1498), an allegorical satire on court intrigue. Skelton also penned intemperate satiri-cal invectives, such as *Collyn Clout* and *Why Come Ye Not to Court?* (both 1522), and reflexive essays on the role of the poet and poetry, in *Speak, Parrot* (written 1521) and *The Garland of Laurel* (1523).

The first half of the 16th century was also a notable period for courtly lyric verse in the stricter sense of poems with musical settings, such as those found in the Devonshire Manuscript. This is very much the literary milieu of the "courtly makers" Sir Thomas Wyatt and Henry Howard, earl of Surrey, but, though the courtly context of much of their writing is of medieval origin, their most distinctive achievements look to the future. Poems such as Wyatt's "They flee from me" and "Whoso list to hunt" vibrate with personal feeling at odds with the medieval convention of anonymity, while Surrey's translations from the *Aeneid* introduce blank verse (unrhymed iambic pentameter) into English for the first time, providing an essential foundation for the achievements of Shakespeare and John Milton.

SIGNIFICANT MIDDLE ENGLISH LITERARY FIGURES

No discussion of Middle English literature would be complete without highlighting some of the most influential and notable authors of this period. Geoffrey Chaucer looms over the Middle English period as its most dominant figure, but this era also produced the first English printer, William Caxton. Both men had a significant influence on English literature.

WILLIAM CAXTON
(b. *c.* 1422, Kent, Eng.—d. 1491, London)

William Caxton was the first English printer. As a translator and publisher, he exerted an important influence on English literature.

In 1438 he was apprenticed to Robert Large, a rich mercer, who in the following year became lord mayor of London. Large died in 1441, and Caxton moved to Brugge, the centre of the European wool trade; during the next 30 years he became an increasingly prosperous and influential member of the English trading community in Flanders and Holland. In 1463 he took up duties as "Governor of the English Nation of Merchant Adventurers" in the Low Countries—a post of real authority over his fellow merchants. Sometime in 1470 he ceased to be governor and

William Caxton—depicted as seated, fatigued from copying translated text by hand—learned the printing trade and became the first English printer. As a publisher, he made a vast array of literature available to the general public. Hulton Archive/Getty Images

entered the service of Margaret, duchess of Burgundy, possibly as her financial adviser.

In that period Caxton's interests were turning to literature. In March 1469 he had begun to translate Raoul Le Fèvre's *Recueil des histoires de Troye*, which he laid aside and did not finish until Sept. 19, 1471. In Cologne, where he lived from 1470 to the end of 1472, he learned printing. In the epilogue of Book III of the completed translation, entitled *The Recuyell of the Historyes of Troye*, he tells how his "pen became worn, his hand weary, his eye dimmed" with copying the book. So he "practised and learnt" at great personal cost how to print it. He set up a press in Brugge about 1474, and the *Recuyell*, the first book printed in English, was published there in 1475. Caxton's translation from the

French of *The Game and Playe of the Chesse* (in which chess is treated as an allegory of life) was published in 1476. Caxton printed two or three other works in Brugge in French, but toward the end of 1476 he returned to England and established his press at Westminster. From then on he devoted himself to writing and printing. The first dated book printed in English, *Dictes and Sayenges of the Phylosophers*, appeared on Nov. 18, 1477.

Although a pioneer of printing in England, Caxton showed no great typographical originality and produced no books of remarkable beauty. Kings, nobles, and rich merchants were Caxton's patrons and sometimes commissioned special books. His varied output—including books of chivalric romance, conduct, morality, history, and philosophy and an encyclopaedia, *The Myrrour of the Worlde* (1481), the first illustrated English book—shows that he catered also to a general public. The large number of service books and devotional works published by Caxton were the staple reading of most literate persons. He also printed nearly all the English literature available to him in his time: *Canterbury Tales* (1478? and 1484?) and other poems by Chaucer, John Gower's *Confessio amantis* (1483), Sir Thomas Malory's *Morte Darthur* (1485), and much of John Lydgate. Caxton translated 24 books, some of them immensely long. By the time of his death, he had published about 100 items of various kinds.

GEOFFREY CHAUCER

(b. *c.* 1342/43, London?, Eng.—d. Oct. 25, 1400, London)

The Canterbury Tales of Geoffrey Chaucer ranks as one of the greatest poetic works in English. He also contributed importantly in the second half of the 14th century to the management of public affairs as courtier, diplomat, and civil servant. In that career he was trusted and aided by

Geoffrey Chaucer, oil on vellum, portrait miniature from Thomas Hoccleve's The Regimen of Princes *(1411; Harley Ms. 4866), in the British Museum.* Courtesy of the trustees of the British Museum

three successive kings—Edward III, Richard II, and Henry IV. But it is his avocation—the writing of poetry—for which he is remembered.

Perhaps the chief characteristics of Chaucer's works are their variety in subject matter, genre, tone, and style and in the complexities presented concerning the human pursuit of a sensible existence. Yet his writings also consistently reflect an all-pervasive humour combined with serious and tolerant consideration of important philosophical questions. From his writings Chaucer emerges as poet of love, both earthly and divine, whose presentations range from lustful cuckoldry to spiritual union with God. Thereby, they regularly lead the reader to speculation about man's relation both to his fellows and to his Maker, while simultaneously providing delightfully entertaining views of the frailties and follies, as well as the nobility, of mankind.

FOREBEARS AND EARLY YEARS

Chaucer's forebears for at least four generations were middle-class English people whose connection with London and the court had steadily increased. John Chaucer, his father, was an important London vintner and a deputy to the king's butler. In 1338 he was a member of Edward III's expedition to Antwerp, in Flanders, now part of Belgium, and he owned property in Ipswich, in the county of Suffolk, and in London. He died in 1366 or 1367 at age 53. The name Chaucer is derived from the French word chaussier, meaning a maker of footwear. The family's financial success derived from wine and leather.

Although c. 1340 is customarily given as Chaucer's birth date, 1342 or 1343 is probably a closer guess. No information exists concerning his early education, although doubtless he would have been as fluent in French as in the Middle English of his time. He also became competent in Latin and Italian. His writings show his close familiarity with many important books of his time and of earlier times.

Chaucer first appears in the records in 1357, as a member of the household of Elizabeth, countess of Ulster, wife of Lionel, third son of Edward III. Geoffrey's father presumably had been able to place him among the group of young men and women serving in that royal household, a customary arrangement whereby families who could do so provided their children with opportunity for the necessary courtly education and connections to advance their careers. By 1359 Chaucer was a member of Edward III's army in France and was captured during the unsuccessful siege of Reims. The king contributed to his ransom, and Chaucer served as messenger from Calais to England during the peace negotiations of 1360. Chaucer does not appear in any contemporary record during 1361–65. He was probably in the king's service, but he may have been studying law—not unusual preparation for public service, then as now—since a 16th-century report implies that, while so engaged, he was fined for beating a Franciscan friar in a London street. On Feb. 22, 1366, the king of Navarre issued a certificate of safe-conduct for Chaucer, three companions, and their servants to enter Spain. This occasion is the first of a number of diplomatic missions to the continent of Europe over the succeeding 10 years, and the wording of the document suggests that here Chaucer served as "chief of mission."

By 1366 Chaucer had married. Probably his wife was Philippa Pan, who had been in the service of the countess of Ulster and entered the service of Philippa of Hainaut, queen consort of Edward III, when Elizabeth died in 1363. In 1366 Philippa Chaucer received an annuity, and later annuities were frequently paid to her through her husband. These and other facts indicate that Chaucer married well.

In 1367 Chaucer received an annuity for life as yeoman of the king, and in the next year he was listed among the king's esquires. Such officers lived at court and performed staff duties of considerable importance. In 1368 Chaucer was abroad on a diplomatic mission, and in 1369 he was on military service in France. Also in 1369 he and his wife were official mourners for the death of Queen Philippa.

Obviously, Chaucer's career was prospering, and his first important poem—*Book of the Duchess*—seems further evidence of his connection with persons in high places.

That poem of more than 1,300 lines, probably written in late 1369 or early 1370, is an elegy for Blanche, duchess of Lancaster, John of Gaunt's first wife, who died of plague in September 1369. Chaucer's close relationship with John, which continued through most of his life, may have commenced as early as Christmas 1357 when they, both about the same age, were present at the countess of Ulster's residence in Yorkshire. For this first of his important poems, Chaucer used the dream-vision form, a genre made popular by the highly influential 13th-century French poem of courtly love, the *Roman de la rose*. Chaucer translated that poem, at least in part, probably as one of his first literary efforts, and he borrowed from it throughout his poetic career. The *Duchess* is also indebted to contemporary French poetry and to Ovid, Chaucer's favourite Roman poet. Nothing in these borrowings, however, will account for his originality in combining dream-vision with elegy and eulogy of Blanche with consolation for John. Also noteworthy here—as it increasingly became in his later poetry—is the tactful and subtle use of a first-person narrator, who both is and is not the poet himself. The device had obvious advantages for the minor courtier delivering such a poem orally before the high-ranking court group. In addition, the *Duchess* foreshadows Chaucer's skill at presenting the rhythms of natural conversation within the confines of Middle English verse and at creating realistic characters within courtly poetic conventions. Also, Chaucer here begins, with the Black Knight's account of his love for Good Fair White, his career as a love poet, examining in late medieval fashion the important philosophic and religious questions concerning the human condition as they relate to both temporal and eternal aspects of love.

DIPLOMAT AND CIVIL SERVANT

During the decade of the 1370s, Chaucer was at various times on diplomatic missions in Flanders, France, and Italy. Probably his first Italian journey (December 1372 to May 1373) was for negotiations with the Genoese concerning an English port for their commerce, and with the Florentines concerning loans for Edward III. His next Italian journey occupied May 28 to Sept. 19, 1378, when he was a member of a mission to Milan concerning military matters. Several times during the 1370s, Chaucer and his wife received generous monetary grants from the king and from John of Gaunt. On May 10, 1374, he obtained rent-free a dwelling above Aldgate, in London, and on June 8 of that year he was appointed comptroller of the customs and subsidy of wools, skins, and tanned hides for the Port of London. Now, for the first time, Chaucer had a position away from the court, and he and his wife had a home of their own, about a 10-minute walk from his office. In 1375 he was granted two wardships, which paid well, and in 1376 he received a sizable sum from a fine. When Richard II became king in June 1377, he confirmed Chaucer's comptrollership and, later, the annuities granted by Edward III to both Geoffrey and Philippa. Certainly during the 1370s fortune smiled upon the Chaucers.

So much responsibility and activity in public matters appears to have left Chaucer little time for writing during this decade. The great literary event for him was that, during his missions to Italy, he encountered the work of Dante, Petrarch, and Boccaccio, which was later to have profound influence upon his own writing. Chaucer's most important work of the 1370s was *Hous of Fame*, a poem of more than 2,000 lines, also in dream-vision form. In some ways it is a failure—it is unfinished, its theme is unclear, and the diversity of its parts seems to overshadow any unity of purpose—but it gives considerable evidence of Chaucer's advancing skill as a poet. The eight-syllable metre is handled with great flexibility; the light, bantering, somewhat ironic tone—later to become one of Chaucer's chief effects—is established; and a wide variety of subject matter is included. Further, the later mastery in creation of memorable characters is here foreshadowed by the marvelous golden eagle who carries the frightened narrator, "Geoffrey," high above the Earth to the houses of Fame and Rumour, so that as a reward for his writing and studying he can learn "tydings" to make into love poems. Here, too, Chaucer's standard picture of his own fictional character emerges: the poet, somewhat dull-witted, dedicated to writing about love but without successful personal experience of it. The comedy of the poem reaches its high point when the pedantic eagle delivers for Geoffrey's edification a learned lecture on the properties of sound. In addition to its comic aspects, however, the poem seems to convey a serious note: like all earthly things, fame is transitory and capricious.

THE MIDDLE YEARS: POLITICAL AND PERSONAL ANXIETIES

In a deed of May 1, 1380, one Cecily Chaumpaigne released Chaucer from legal action, "both of my rape and of any other matter or cause." Rape (raptus) could at the time mean either sexual assault or abduction. Scholars have not been able to establish which meaning applies here, but, in either case, the release suggests that Chaucer was not guilty as charged. He continued to work at the Customs House and in 1382 was additionally appointed comptroller of the petty customs for wine and other merchandise, but in October 1386 his dwelling in London was leased to another man, and in December of that year successors were named for both of his comptrollerships in the customs. Whether he resigned or was removed from office is not clear. Between 1382 and 1386 he had arranged for deputies—permanent in two instances and temporary in others—in his work at the customs. In October 1385 he was appointed a justice of the peace for Kent, and in August 1386 he became knight of the shire for Kent, to attend Parliament in October. Further, in 1385 he probably moved to Greenwich, then in Kent, to live. These circumstances suggest that, for some time before 1386, he was planning to move from London and to leave the Customs House. Philippa Chaucer apparently died in 1387. If she had suffered poor health for some time previously, that situation could have influenced a decision to move. On the other hand, political circumstances during this period were not favourable for Chaucer and may have caused his removal. By 1386 a baronial group led by Thomas of Woodstock, duke of Gloucester, had bested both Richard II and John of Gaunt—with whose parties Chaucer had long been associated—and usurped the king's authority and administration. Numerous other officeholders—like Chaucer, appointed by the king—were discharged, and Chaucer may have suffered similarly. Perhaps the best view of the matter is that Chaucer saw which way the political wind was blowing and began early to prepare to move when the necessity arrived.

The period 1386–89 was clearly difficult for Chaucer. Although he was reappointed justice of the peace for 1387, he was not returned to Parliament after 1386. In 1387 he was granted protection for a year to go to Calais, in France, but seems not to have gone, perhaps because of his wife's death. In 1388 a series of suits against him for debts began, and he sold his royal pension for a lump sum. Also, from February

3 to June 4, 1388, the Merciless Parliament, controlled by the barons, caused many leading members of the court party—some of them Chaucer's close friends—to be executed. In May 1389, however, the 23-year-old King Richard II regained control, ousted his enemies, and began appointing his supporters to office. Almost certainly, Chaucer owed his next public office to that political change. On July 12, 1389, he was appointed clerk of the king's works, with executive responsibility for repair and maintenance of royal buildings, such as the Tower of London and Westminster Palace, and with a comfortable salary.

Although political events of the 1380s, from the Peasants' Revolt of 1381 through the Merciless Parliament of 1388, must have kept Chaucer steadily anxious, he produced a sizable body of writings during this decade, some of very high order. Surprisingly, these works do not in any way reflect the tense political scene. Indeed, one is tempted to speculate that during this period Chaucer turned to his reading and writing as escape from the difficulties of his public life. *The Parlement of Foules*, a poem of 699 lines, is a dream-vision for St. Valentine's Day, making use of the myth that each year on that day the birds gathered before the goddess Nature to choose their mates. Beneath its playfully humorous tone, it seems to examine the value of various kinds of love within the context of "common profit" as set forth in the introductory abstract from the *Somnium Scipionis* (*The Dream of Scipio*) of Cicero. The narrator searches unsuccessfully for an answer and concludes that he must continue his search in other books. For this poem Chaucer also borrowed extensively from Boccaccio and Dante, but the lively bird debate from which the poem takes its title is for the most part original. The poem has often been taken as connected with events at court, particularly the marriage in 1382 of Richard II and Anne of Bohemia. But no such connection has ever been firmly established. The *Parlement* is clearly the best of Chaucer's earlier works.

The *Consolation of Philosophy*, written by the Roman philosopher Boethius (early 6th century), a Christian, was one of the most influential of medieval books. Its discussion of free will, God's foreknowledge, destiny, fortune, and true and false happiness—in effect, all aspects of the manner in which the right-minded individual should direct his thinking and action to gain eternal salvation—had a deep and lasting effect upon Chaucer's thought and art. His prose translation of the *Consolation* is carefully done, and in his next poem—*Troilus and Criseyde*—the influence of Boethius's book is pervasive. Chaucer took the basic plot for this 8,239-line poem from Boccaccio's *Filostrato*.

Some critics consider *Troilus and Criseyde* Chaucer's finest work, greater even than the far more widely read *Canterbury Tales*. But the two works are so different that comparative evaluation seems fruitless. The state of the surviving manuscripts of *Troilus* shows Chaucer's detailed effort in revising this poem. Against the background of the legendary Trojan War, the love story of Troilus, son of the Trojan king Priam, and Criseyde, widowed daughter of the deserter priest Calkas, is recounted. The poem moves in leisurely fashion, with introspection and much of what would now be called psychological insight dominating many sections. Aided by Criseyde's uncle Pandarus, Troilus and Criseyde are united in love about halfway through the poem, but then she is sent to join her father in the Greek camp outside Troy. Despite her promise to return, she gives her love to the Greek Diomede, and Troilus, left in despair, is killed in the war. These events are interspersed with Boethian discussion of free will and determinism. At the end of the poem, when Troilus's soul rises into the heavens, the folly of complete immersion in sexual love is viewed in relation to the eternal love of God. The effect of the poem is controlled throughout by the direct comments of the narrator, whose sympathy for the lovers—especially for Criseyde—is ever present.

Also in the 1380s Chaucer produced his fourth and final dream-vision poem, *The Legend of Good Women*, which is not a success. It presents a Prologue, existing in two versions, and nine stories. In the Prologue the god of love is angry because Chaucer had earlier written about so many women who betrayed men. As penance, Chaucer must now write about good women. The Prologue is noteworthy for the delightful humour of the narrator's self-mockery and for the passages in praise of books and of the spring. The stories—concerning such women of antiquity as Cleopatra, Dido, and Lucrece—are brief and rather mechanical, with the betrayal of women by wicked men as a regular theme. As a result, the whole becomes more a legend of bad men than of good women. Perhaps the most important fact about the *Legend*, however, is that it shows Chaucer structuring a long poem as a collection of stories within a framework. Seemingly the static nature of the framing device for the *Legend* and the repetitive aspect of the series of stories with a single theme led him to give up this attempt as a poor job. But the failure here must have contributed to his brilliant choice, probably about this same time, of a pilgrimage as the framing device for the stories in *The Canterbury Tales*.

LAST YEARS AND THE CANTERBURY TALES

Chaucer's service as clerk of the king's works lasted only from July 1389 to June 1391. During that tenure he was robbed several times and once beaten, sufficient reason for seeking a change of jobs. In June 1391 he was appointed sub-forester of the king's park in North Petherton, Somerset, an office that he held until his death. He retained his home

Geoffrey Chaucer, from the 15th-century Ellesmere manuscript of The Canterbury Tales. *Photos.com/Jupiterimages*

relationship during 1395–96 with John of Gaunt's son, the earl of Derby, later King Henry IV. When John died in February 1399, King Richard confiscated John's Lancastrian inheritance. Then in May he set forth to crush the Irish revolt. In so doing, he left his country ready to rebel. Henry, exiled in 1398 but now duke of Lancaster, returned to England to claim his rights. The people flocked to him, and he was crowned on Sept. 30, 1399. He confirmed Chaucer's grants from Richard II and in October added an additional generous annuity. In December 1399 Chaucer took a lease on a house in the garden of Westminster Abbey. But in October of the following year he died. He was buried in the Abbey, a signal honour for a commoner.

Chaucer's great literary accomplishment of the 1390s was *The Canterbury Tales*. In it a group of about 30 pilgrims gather at the Tabard Inn in Southwark, across the Thames from London, and agree to engage in a storytelling contest as they travel on horseback to the shrine of Thomas à Becket in Canterbury, Kent, and back. Harry Bailly, host of the Tabard, serves as master of ceremonies for the contest. The pilgrims are introduced by vivid brief sketches in the General Prologue. Interspersed between the 24 tales told by the pilgrims are short dramatic scenes presenting lively exchanges, called links and usually involving the host and one or more of the pilgrims. Chaucer did not complete the full plan for his book; the return journey from Canterbury is not included, and some of the pilgrims do not tell stories. Further, the surviving manuscripts leave room for doubt at some points as to Chaucer's intent for arranging the material. The work is nevertheless sufficiently complete to be considered a unified book rather than a collection of unfinished fragments.

Use of a pilgrimage as a framing device for the collection of stories enabled Chaucer to bring together people from many walks of life: knight, prioress, monk; merchant, man of law, franklin, scholarly clerk; miller, reeve, pardoner; wife of Bath; and many others. Also, the pilgrimage and the storytelling contest allowed presentation of a highly varied collection of literary genres: courtly romance, racy fabliau, saint's life, allegorical tale, beast fable, medieval sermon, alchemical account, and, at times, mixtures of these genres. Because of this structure, the sketches, the links, and the tales all fuse as complex presentations of the pilgrims, while at the same time the tales present remarkable examples of short stories in verse, plus two expositions in prose. In addition, the pilgrimage, combining a fundamentally religious purpose with its secular aspect of vacation in the spring, made possible extended consideration of the relationship between the pleasures and vices of this world and the spiritual aspirations for the next, that seeming dichotomy with which Chaucer, like Boethius and many other medieval writers, was so steadily concerned.

For this crowning glory of his 30 years of literary composition, Chaucer used his wide and deep study of medieval books of many sorts and his acute observation of daily life at many levels. He also employed his detailed knowledge of medieval astrology and subsidiary sciences as they were thought to influence and dictate human behaviour. Over the whole expanse of this intricate dramatic narrative, he presides as Chaucer the poet, Chaucer the civil servant, and Chaucer the pilgrim, somewhat slow-witted in his pose and always intrigued by human frailty but always questioning the complexity of the human condition and always seeing both the humour and the tragedy in that condition. At the end, in the Retractation with which *The Canterbury Tales* closes, Chaucer as poet and pilgrim states his conclusion that the concern for this world fades into insignificance before the prospect for the next. In view of the admonitions in

"The Parson's Tale," he asks forgiveness for his writings that concern "worldly vanities" and remembrance for his translation of the *Consolation* and his other works of morality and religious devotion. On that note he ends his finest work and his career as poet.

Information concerning Chaucer's children is not fully clear. The probability is that he and Philippa had two sons and two daughters. One son, Thomas Chaucer, who died in 1434, owned large tracts of land and held important offices in the 1420s, including the forestership of North Petherton. He later leased Chaucer's house in Westminster, and his twice-widowed daughter Alice became duchess of Suffolk. In 1391 Chaucer had written *Treatise on the Astrolabe* for "little Lewis," probably his younger son, then 10 years old. Elizabeth "Chaucy," probably the poet's daughter, was a nun at Barking in 1381. A second probable daughter, Agnes Chaucer, was a lady-in-waiting at Henry IV's coronation in 1399. The records lend some support to speculation that John of Gaunt fathered one or more of these children. Chaucer seems to have had no descendants living after the 15th century.

JOHN GOWER
(b. 1330? — d. 1408, London?, Eng.)

John Gower was a medieval English poet who worked in the tradition of courtly love and moral allegory. He strongly influenced the writing of other poets of his day and once had a reputation that matched that of his contemporary and friend Geoffrey Chaucer. After the 16th century, however, his popularity waned, and interest in him did not revive until the middle of the 20th century.

It is thought from Gower's language that he was of Kentish origin, though his family may have come from

Yorkshire, and he was clearly a man of some wealth. Allusions in his poetry and other documents, however, indicate that he knew London well and was probably a court official. At one point, he professed acquaintance with Richard II, and in 1399 he was granted two pipes (casks) of wine a year for life by Henry IV as a reward for complimentary references in one of his poems. In 1397, living as a layman in the priory of St. Mary Overie, Southwark, London, Gower married Agnes Groundolf, who survived him. In 1400 Gower described himself as "senex et cecus" ("old and blind"), and on Oct. 24, 1408, his will was proved. He left bequests to the Southwark priory, where he is buried.

Gower's three major works are in French, English, and Latin, and he also wrote a series of French *balades* intended for the English court. The *Speculum meditantis,* or *Mirour de l'omme,* in French, is composed of 12-line stanzas and opens impressively with a description of the devil's marriage to the seven daughters of sin. Continuing with the marriage of reason and the seven virtues, it ends with a searing examination of the sins of English society just before the Peasants' Revolt of 1381: the denunciatory tone is relieved at the very end by a long hymn to the Virgin.

Gower's major Latin poem, the *Vox clamantis,* owes much to Ovid. It is essentially a homily, being in part a criticism of the three estates of society, in part a mirror for a prince, in elegiac form. The poet's political doctrines are traditional, but he uses the Latin language with fluency and elegance.

Gower's English poems include *In Praise of Peace,* in which he pleads urgently with the king to avoid the horrors of war, but his greatest English work is the *Confessio amantis,* essentially a collection of exemplary tales of love, whereby Venus' priest, Genius, instructs the poet, Amans, in the art of both courtly and Christian love. The stories are chiefly adapted from classical and medieval sources and are told with a tenderness and the restrained narrative art that constitute Gower's main appeal today.

LAWAMON
(fl. 12th century)

Lawamon, an early Middle English poet, was the author of the romance-chronicle the *Brut* (c. 1200), one of the most notable English poems of the 12th century. It is the first work in English to treat of the "matter of Britain"—i.e., the legends surrounding Arthur and the knights of the Round Table—and was written at a time when English was nearly eclipsed by French and Latin as a literary language.

Lawamon (also spelled Layamon or Laghamon) describes himself as a priest living at Arley Kings in Worcestershire. His source was the *Roman de Brut* by Wace, an Anglo-Norman verse adaptation of Geoffrey of Monmouth's *History of the Kings of Britain*. In about 16,000 long alliterative lines (often broken into short couplets by rhyme), the *Brut* relates the legendary history of Britain from the landing of Brutus, great-grandson of the Trojan Aeneas, to the final Saxon victory over the Britons in 689. One-third of the poem deals with Arthurian matter, but Lawamon's is not a high chivalric treatment: mass war is the staple, with Arthur the splendid war leader of Germanic tradition.

ROBERT MANNYNG
(b. c. 1330)

The early English poet Robert Mannyng of Brunne was the author of *Handlyng Synne*, a confessional manual, and of the chronicle *Story of England*. The works are preserved independently in several manuscripts, none of certain provenance.

The author is probably to be identified with a Sir Robert de Brunne, chaplain, named as executor in a Lincoln will of 1327. Apart from this mention, his biography can be reconstructed only from his writings. He was at the University of Cambridge around 1300. For 15 years (*c.* 1302–*c.* 1317) Mannyng was a Gilbertine canon at Sempringham priory, Lincolnshire, where in 1303 he began *Handlyng Synne* and was still working at it after 1307. For many years he was engaged on the *Story of England*, which, he relates, was finished between 3 and 4 o'clock, on Friday, May 15, 1338.

Handlyng Synne is an adaptation in about 13,000 lines, in short couplets poorly versified, of the *Manuel des Péchés* ("Handbook of Sins"), which is usually ascribed to William of Waddington (or Widdington), an Englishman, probably a Yorkshireman, writing in Anglo-Norman between 1250 and 1270. Like Waddington, Mannyng aimed to provide a handbook intended to stimulate careful self-examination as preparation for confession.

Mannyng deals in turn with the Ten Commandments, the seven deadly sins and the sin of sacrilege, the seven sacraments, the 12 requisites of confession, and the 12 graces of confession. There is much direct instruction, exhortation, and didactic comment. Each of the topics is illustrated by one or more tales. These exempla have sometimes been considered to provide the particular interest of the work. The whole work is designed for oral delivery. Mannyng's merit as a storyteller lies in his apt management of material and in his lucid, direct narration. Otherwise the literary merits of *Handlyng Synne* are negligible, although its documentary value for social history is great. It illustrates clearly the attitudes and values of the English minor clergy and peasantry in the early 14th century. Throughout there is much comment on the social, domestic, parochial, and commercial scene.

Of similar literary quality is Mannyng's later work, the *Story of England*, but the basis of the *Story of England* is fiction. As history it is almost worthless. The work falls into two parts. The first tells the story from the biblical Noah to the death of the British king Caedwalla in 689. In the second part, he takes the story to the death of Edward I (1307).

Of particular interest is his incorporation of elements of popular romance, such as the story of Guy of Warwick's encounter with the giant Colbrand, which he inserts into his account of Athelstan. He works into his narrative several topical songs, mainly on the Scottish wars of Edward I's time.

ORM
(fl. *c.* 1200)

Orm (also called Ormin) was an Augustinian canon who wrote an early Middle English book of metrical homilies on the Gospels, to which he gave the title *Ormulum*, "because Orm made it." The work (dated on linguistic evidence *c.* 1200) is of little literary interest but of great value to linguists, for Orm—who clearly wished to spread sound teaching, derived mainly from works of Gregory the Great, Bede, and Aelfric—invented an individual and remarkably consistent orthography based on phonetic principles. Intended to help preachers when reading his work aloud, it shows, for example, the quantity (length) of the vowels by doubling a consonant after a short vowel in a closed syllable, and it distinguishes by three separate symbols sounds that in the Anglo-Celtic or insular script of Old English were all represented by a single symbol.

RICHARD ROLLE

(b. *c.* 1300, Thornton, Yorkshire [now in North Yorkshire], Eng.—d.
Sept. 29, 1349, Hampole, Yorkshire [now in South Yorkshire])

Richard Rolle de Hampole was an English mystic and author of mystical and ascetic tracts.

Rolle attended the University of Oxford but, dissatisfied with the subjects of study and the disputatiousness there, left without a degree. He established himself as a hermit on the estate of John Dalton of Pickering, but he later moved to other hermitages and probably always led a wandering life, rousing some opposition but winning much admiration. He kept in touch with a number of religious communities in the north and seems to have become spiritual adviser to the nuns at Hampole, in south Yorkshire, before his death there.

Rolle's importance lies in the devotional prose he composed in the vernacular for women readers. It is sometimes difficult to distinguish his writings from those of his followers and imitators. Those English or Latin epistles and treatises that have definitely been attributed to Rolle, however, reflect his fervent devotion and his emphasis on a rapturous mystical union with God. Throughout his writings the life of contemplation and solitude is exalted. Rolle's writings in Latin are overly rhetorical, but his English prose style is lively, flexible, and persuasive. His influence and reputation lasted until the Protestant Reformation.

CHAPTER 3

THE RENAISSANCE PERIOD (1550–1660)

B y the end of the Middle English period, the ground-work was laid for the remarkable writing of the Renaissance. In a tradition of literature notable for its exacting and brilliant achievements, the Elizabethan and early Stuart periods have been said to represent the most brilliant century of all. (The reign of Elizabeth I began in 1558 and ended with her death in 1603. She was succeeded by the Stuart king James VI of Scotland, who took the title James I of England as well. English literature of his reign as James I, from 1603 to 1625, is properly called Jacobean.) These years produced a gallery of authors of genius, some of whom have never been surpassed, and conferred on scores of lesser talents the enviable ability to write with fluency, imagination, and verve. From one point of view, this sudden renaissance looks radiant, confident, heroic—and belated, but all the more dazzling for its belatedness. Yet, from another point of view, this was a time of unusually traumatic strain, in which English society underwent massive disruptions that transformed it on every front and decisively affected the life of every individual. In the brief, intense moment in which England assimilated the European Renaissance, the circumstances that made the assimilation possible were already disintegrating and calling into question the newly won certainties, as well as the older truths that they were dislodging. This doubleness, of new possibilities and new doubts simultaneously apprehended, gives the literature its unrivaled intensity.

SOCIAL CONDITIONS

In this period England's population doubled, prices rocketed, rents followed, old social loyalties dissolved, and new industrial, agricultural, and commercial veins were first tapped. Real wages hit an all-time low in the 1620s, and social relations were plunged into a state of fluidity from which the merchant and the ambitious lesser gentleman profited at the expense of the aristocrat and the labourer, as satires and comedies current from the 1590s complain. Behind the Elizabethan vogue for pastoral poetry lies the fact of the prosperity of the enclosing sheep farmer, who sought to increase pasture at the expense of the peasantry. Tudor platitudes about order and degree could neither combat nor survive the challenge posed to rank by these arrivistes. The position of the crown, politically dominant yet financially insecure, had always been potentially unstable, and, when Charles I lost the confidence of his greater subjects in the 1640s, his authority crumbled. Meanwhile, the huge body of poor fell ever further behind the rich. The pamphlets of Thomas Harman (1566) and Robert Greene (1591–92), as well as William Shakespeare's *King Lear* (1605–06), provide glimpses of a horrific world of vagabondage and crime, the Elizabethans' biggest, unsolvable social problem.

INTELLECTUAL AND RELIGIOUS REVOLUTION

The barely disguised social ferment was accompanied by an intellectual revolution, as the medieval synthesis collapsed before the new science, new religion, and new humanism. While modern mechanical technologies were pressed into service by the Stuarts to create the scenic wonders of the court masque, the discoveries of astronomers and explorers were redrawing the cosmos in a way that was profoundly disturbing:

> *And freely men confess that this world's spent,*
> *When in the planets, and the firmament*
> *They seek so many new....*

(John Donne, *The First Anniversary*, 1611)

The majority of people were more immediately affected by the religious revolutions of the 16th century. A person in early adulthood at the accession of Elizabeth in 1558 would, by her death in 1603, have been vouchsafed an unusually disillusioning insight into the duty owed by private conscience to the needs of the state. The Tudor church hierarchy was an instrument of social and political control, yet the mid-century controversies over the faith had already wrecked any easy confidence in the authority of doctrines and forms and had taught people to inquire carefully into the rationale of their own beliefs (as John Donne does in his third satire [c. 1596]). The Elizabethan ecclesiastical compromise was the object of continual criticism, from radicals both within (who desired progressive reforms, such as the abolition of bishops) and without (who desired the return of England to the Roman Catholic fold), but the incipient liberalism of individuals such as John Milton and the scholar and churchman William Chillingworth was held in check by the majority's unwillingness to tolerate a plurality of religions in a supposedly unitary state. Nor was the Calvinist orthodoxy that cradled most English writers comforting, for it told them that they were corrupt, unfree, unable to earn their own salvations, and subject to heavenly judgments that were arbitrary and absolute. Calvinism deeply affects the world of the Jacobean tragedies, whose heroes are not masters of their fates but victims of divine purposes that are terrifying yet inscrutable.

THE RACE FOR CULTURAL DEVELOPMENT

Another complicating factor was the race to catch up with Continental developments in arts and philosophy. The Tudors needed to create a class of educated diplomats, statesmen, and officials and to dignify their court by making it a fount of cultural as well as political patronage. The new learning, widely disseminated through the Erasmian (after the humanist Desiderius Erasmus) educational programs of such men as John Colet and Sir Thomas Elyot, proposed to use a systematic schooling in Latin authors and some Greek to encourage in the social elites a flexibility of mind and civilized serviceableness that would allow enlightened princely government to walk hand in hand with responsible scholarship.

Humanism fostered an intimate familiarity with the classics that was a powerful incentive for the creation of an English literature of answerable dignity, as well a practical, secular piety that left its impress everywhere on Elizabethan writing. Humanism's effect, however, was modified by the simultaneous impact of the flourishing Continental cultures, particularly the Italian. Repeatedly, crucial innovations in English letters developed resources originating from Italy—such as the sonnet of Petrarch, the epic of Ludovico Ariosto, the pastoral of Jacopo Sannazaro, the canzone, and blank verse—and values imported with these forms were in competition with the humanists' ethical preoccupations. Social ideals of

Ideas and attitudes put forth by the Italian courtier Baldassare Castiglione in his Il cortegiano *permeated Elizabethan court poetry as the English attempted to bring cultural refinement to their literature.* Hulton Archive/ Getty Images

wit, many-sidedness, and sprezzatura (accomplishment mixed with unaffectedness) were imbibed from Baldassare Castiglione's *Il cortegiano*, translated as *The Courtyer* by Sir Thomas Hoby in 1561. Elizabethan court poetry is steeped in Castiglione's aristocratic Neoplatonism, his notions of universal proportion, and the love of beauty as the path to virtue.

Equally significant was the welcome afforded to Niccolò Machiavelli, whose lessons were vilified publicly and absorbed in private. *The Prince*, written in 1513, was unavailable in English until 1640, but as early as the 1580s Gabriel Harvey, a friend of the poet Edmund Spenser, can be found enthusiastically hailing its author as the apostle of modern pragmatism. "We are much beholden to Machiavel and others," said Francis Bacon, "that write what men do, and not what they ought to do."

So the literary revival occurred in a society rife with tensions, uncertainties, and competing versions of order and authority, religion and status, sex and the self. The Elizabethan settlement was a compromise. The Tudor pretense that the people of England were unified in belief disguised the actual fragmentation of the old consensus under the strain of change. The new scientific knowledge proved both man's littleness and his power to command nature. Against the Calvinist idea of man's helplessness pulled the humanist faith in his dignity, especially that conviction, derived from the reading of Seneca and so characteristic of the period, of man's constancy and fortitude, his heroic capacity for self-determination. It was still possible for Elizabeth to hold these divergent tendencies together in a single, heterogeneous culture, but under her successors they would eventually fly apart. The philosophers speaking for the new century would be Francis Bacon, who argued for the gradual advancement of science through patient accumulation of experiments, and the skeptic Michel de Montaigne (his *Essays* translated from the French by John Florio [1603]), who denied that it was possible to formulate any general principles of knowledge.

Cutting across all of these was the persistence of popular habits of thought and expression. Both humanism and

Puritanism set themselves against vulgar ignorance and folk tradition, but, fortunately, neither could remain aloof for long from the robustness of popular taste. Sir Philip Sidney, in England's first Neoclassical literary treatise, *The Defence of Poesie* (written *c.* 1578–83, published 1595), candidly admitted that "the old song [i.e., ballad] of Percy and Douglas" would move his heart "more than with a trumpet," and his *Arcadia* (final version published in 1593) is a representative instance of the fruitful cross-fertilization of genres in this period—the contamination of aristocratic pastoral with popular tale, the lyric with the ballad, comedy with romance, tragedy with satire, and poetry with prose.

The language, too, was undergoing a rapid expansion that all classes contributed to and benefited from, sophisticated literature borrowing without shame the idioms of colloquial speech. An allusion in Shakespeare's *Macbeth* (1606–07) to heaven peeping "through the blanket of the dark" would become a "problem" only later, when, for instance, Samuel Johnson complained in 1751 that such words provoked laughter rather than awe. Johnson's was an age when tragic dignity implied politeness, when it was below the dignity of tragedy to mention so lowly an object as a blanket. But the Elizabethans' ability to address themselves to several audiences simultaneously and to bring into relation opposed experiences, emphases, and worldviews invested their writing with complexity and power.

ELIZABETHAN POETRY AND PROSE

English poetry and prose burst into sudden glory in the late 1570s. A decisive shift of taste toward a fluent artistry self-consciously displaying its own grace and sophistication was announced in the works of Spenser and Sidney. It was accompanied by an upsurge in literary production that came to fruition in the 1590s and 1600s, two decades of astonishing productivity by writers of every persuasion and calibre.

The groundwork was laid in the 30 years from 1550, a period of slowly increasing confidence in the literary competence of the language and tremendous advances in education, which for the first time produced a substantial English readership, keen for literature and possessing cultivated tastes. This development was underpinned by the technological maturity and accelerating output (mainly in pious or technical subjects) of Elizabethan printing. The Stationers' Company, which controlled the publication of books, was incorporated in 1557, and Richard Tottel's *Miscellany* (1557) revolutionized the relationship of poet and audience by making publicly available lyric poetry, which hitherto had circulated only among a courtly coterie. Spenser was the first significant English poet deliberately to use print to advertise his talents.

DEVELOPMENT OF THE ENGLISH LANGUAGE

The prevailing opinion of the language's inadequacy, its lack of "terms" and innate inferiority to the eloquent Classical tongues, was combated in the work of the humanists Thomas Wilson, Roger Ascham, and Sir John Cheke, whose treatises on rhetoric, education, and even archery argued in favour of an unaffected vernacular prose and a judicious attitude toward linguistic borrowings. Their stylistic ideals are attractively embodied in Ascham's educational tract *The Schoolmaster* (1570), and their tonic effect on that particularly Elizabethan art, translation, can be felt in the earliest important examples, Sir Thomas Hoby's *Castiglione* (1561) and Sir Thomas North's *Plutarch* (1579). A further stimulus was the religious upheaval that took place in the middle of the century. The desire of reformers to address as comprehensive an audience as possible—the bishop and the boy who follows the plough, as William Tyndale put it—produced the first true classics of English prose: the reformed Anglican Book of Common Prayer (1549, 1552, 1559); John Foxe's *Acts and Monuments* (1563), which celebrates the martyrs, great and small, of English Protestantism; and the various English versions of the Bible, from Tyndale's New Testament (1525), Miles Coverdale's Bible (1535), and the Geneva Bible (1560) to the syncretic Authorized Version (or King James's Version, 1611). The latter's combination of grandeur and plainness is justly celebrated, even if it represents an idiom never spoken in heaven or on earth. Nationalism inspired by the Reformation motivated the historical chronicles of the capable and stylish Edward Hall (1548), who bequeathed to Shakespeare the tendentious Tudor interpretation of the 15th century, and of Raphael Holinshed (1577).

In verse, Tottel's much reprinted *Miscellany* generated a series of imitations and, by popularizing the lyrics of Sir Thomas Wyatt and the earl of Surrey, carried into the 1570s the tastes of the early Tudor court. The newer poets collected by Tottel and other anthologists include Nicholas Grimald, Richard Edwardes, George Turberville, Barnabe Googe, George Gascoigne, Sir John Harington, and many others, of whom Gascoigne is the most prominent. The modern preference for the ornamental manner of the next generation has eclipsed these poets, who continued the tradition of plain, weighty verse, addressing themselves to ethical and didactic themes and favouring the meditative lyric, satire, and epigram. But their taste for economy, restraint, and aphoristic density was, in the verse of Donne and Ben Jonson, to outlive the cult of elegance. The period's major project was *A Mirror for Magistrates* (1559; enlarged editions 1563, 1578, 1587), a collection of verse laments, by several hands, purporting to be spoken by participants in the Wars of the Roses and preaching the Tudor doctrine of obedience. The quality is uneven, but Thomas Sackville's *Induction* and Thomas Churchyard's *Legend of Shore's Wife* are distinguished, and the intermingling of history, tragedy, and political morality was to be influential on the drama.

SIR PHILIP SIDNEY AND EDMUND SPENSER

With the work of Sir Philip Sidney and Edmund Spenser, Tottel's contributors suddenly began to look old-fashioned. Sidney epitomized the new Renaissance "universal man," a courtier, diplomat, soldier, and poet whose *Defence of Poesie* includes the first considered account of the state of English letters. Sidney's treatise defends literature on the ground of its unique power to teach, but his real emphasis is on its delight, its ability to depict the world not as it is but as it ought to be. This quality of "forcibleness or energia" he himself demonstrated in his sonnet sequence of unrequited desire, *Astrophel and Stella* (written 1582, published 1591). His *Arcadia*, in its first version (written *c.* 1577–80), is a pastoral romance in which courtiers disguised as Amazons and shepherds make love and sing delicate experimental verses. The revised version (written *c.* 1580–84, published 1590; the last three books of the first version were added in 1593), vastly expanded but abandoned in mid-sentence, added sprawling plots of heroism in love and war, philosophical and political discourses, and set pieces of aristocratic etiquette.

Sidney was a dazzling and assured innovator whose pioneering of new forms and stylistic melody was seminal for his generation. His public fame was as an aristocratic champion of an aggressively Protestant foreign policy, but Elizabeth had no time for idealistic warmongering, and the unresolved conflicts in his poetry—desire against

Among Sir Philip Sidney's works is The Defence of Poesie, *which emphasized English literature's beauty as art, as well as its ability to inform and teach.* Hulton Archive/Getty Images

restraint, heroism against patience, rebellion against submission—mirror his own discomfort with his situation as an unsuccessful courtier.

Protestantism also loomed large in Spenser's life. He enjoyed the patronage of the earl of Leicester, who sought to advance militant Protestantism at court, and his poetic manifesto, *The Shepherds Calendar* (1579), covertly praised

Archbishop Edmund Grindal, who had been suspended by Elizabeth for his Puritan sympathies. Spenser's masterpiece, *The Faerie Queene* (1590–96), is an epic of Protestant nationalism in which the villains are infidels or papists, the hero is King Arthur, and the central value is married chastity.

Spenser was one of the humanistically trained breed of public servants, and the *Calendar*, an expertly crafted collection of pastoral eclogues, both advertised his talents and announced his epic ambitions. The exquisite lyric gift that it reveals was voiced again in the marriage poems *Epithalamion* (1595) and *Prothalamion* (1596). With *The Faerie Queene* he achieved the central poem of the Elizabethan period. Its form fuses the medieval allegory with the Italian romantic epic. Its purpose was "to fashion a gentleman or noble person in virtuous and gentle discipline." The plan was for 12 books (6 were completed), focusing on 12 virtues exemplified in the quests of 12 knights from the court of Gloriana, the Faerie Queene, a symbol of Elizabeth herself. Arthur, in quest of Gloriana's love, would appear in each book and come to exemplify Magnificence, the complete man. Spenser took the decorative chivalry of the Elizabethan court festivals and reworked it through a constantly shifting veil of allegory, so that the knights' adventures and loves build into a complex, multileveled portrayal of the moral life. The verse, a spacious and slow-moving nine-lined stanza, and archaic language frequently rise to an unrivaled sensuousness.

The Faerie Queene was a public poem, addressed to the queen, and politically it echoed the hopes of the Leicester circle for government motivated by godliness and militancy. Spenser's increasing disillusion with the court and with the active life, a disillusion noticeable in the poem's later books and in his bitter satire *Colin Clouts Come Home Again* (1591), voiced the fading of these expectations in

At first a poet preoccupied mainly with patronage, Edmund Spenser became disillusioned with Elizabethan court life. His disenchantment shows in later books of his allegorical poem The Faerie Queene. Archive Photos/ Getty Images

the last decade of Elizabeth's reign, the beginning of that remarkable failure of political and cultural confidence in the monarchy. In the *Mutability Cantos*, melancholy fragments of a projected seventh book (published posthumously in 1609), Spenser turned away from the public world altogether toward the ambiguous consolations of eternity.

The lessons taught by Sidney and Spenser in the cultivation of melodic smoothness and graceful refinement appear to good effect in the subsequent virtuoso outpouring of lyrics and sonnets. These are among the most engaging achievements of the age, though the outpouring was itself partly a product of frustration, as a generation trained to expect office or preferment but faced with courtly parsimony channeled its energies in new directions in search of patronage. For Sidney's fellow courtiers, pastoral and love lyric were also a means of obliquely expressing one's relationship with the queen, of advancing a proposal or an appeal.

ELIZABETHAN LYRIC

Virtually every Elizabethan poet tried his hand at the lyric; few, if any, failed to write one that is not still anthologized today. The fashion for interspersing prose fiction with lyric interludes, begun in the *Arcadia*, was continued by Robert Greene and Thomas Lodge (notably in the latter's *Rosalynde* [1590], the source for Shakespeare's *As You Like It* [c. 1598–1600]), and in the theatres plays of every kind were diversified by songs both popular and courtly. Fine examples are in the plays of Ben Jonson, John Lyly, George Peele, Thomas Nashe, and Thomas Dekker (though all, of course, are outshone by Shakespeare's). The most important influence on lyric poetry, though, was the outstanding richness of late Tudor and Jacobean music, in both the native tradition of expressive lute song, represented by John Dowland and Robert Johnson, and the complex Italianate madrigal newly imported by William Byrd and Thomas Morley.

The foremost talent among lyricists, Thomas Campion, was a composer as well as a poet. His songs (four *Books of Airs*, 1601–17) are unsurpassed for their clarity, harmoniousness, and rhythmic subtlety. Even the work of a lesser talent, however, such as Nicholas Breton, is remarkable for the suggestion of depth and poise in the slightest performances. The smoothness and apparent spontaneity of the Elizabethan lyric conceal a consciously ordered and laboured artifice, attentive to decorum and rhetorical fitness. These are not personal but public pieces, intended for singing and governed by a Neoplatonic aesthetic in which delight is a means of addressing the moral sense, harmonizing and attuning the auditor's mind to the discipline of reason and virtue. This necessitates a deliberate narrowing of scope—to the readily comprehensible situations of pastoral or Petrarchan hope and despair— and makes for a certain uniformity of effect, albeit an agreeable one. The lesser talents are well displayed in the miscellanies *The Phoenix Nest* (1593), *England's Helicon* (1600), and *A Poetical Rhapsody* (1602).

THE SONNET SEQUENCE

The publication of Sidney's *Astrophel and Stella* in 1591 generated an equally extraordinary vogue for the sonnet sequence, Sidney's principal imitators being Samuel Daniel, Michael Drayton, Fulke Greville, Spenser, and Shakespeare. His lesser imitators included Henry Constable, Barnabe Barnes, Giles Fletcher the Elder, Lodge, and Richard Barnfield.

Astrophel had re-created the Petrarchan world of proud beauty and despairing lover in a single, brilliant stroke, though in English hands the preferred division of the sonnet into three quatrains and a couplet gave Petrarch's contemplative form a more forensic turn, investing it with an argumentative terseness and epigrammatic sting. Within the common ground shared by the sequences, there is much diversity. Only Sidney's sequence endeavours to tell a story, the others being more loosely organized as variations focusing on a central (usually fictional) relationship. Daniel's *Delia* (1592) is eloquent and elegant, dignified and high-minded. Drayton's *Ideas Mirror* (1594; much revised by 1619) rises to a strongly imagined, passionate intensity, and Spenser's *Amoretti* (1595) celebrates, unusually, fulfilled sexual love achieved within marriage. Shakespeare's sonnets (published 1609) present a different world altogether, the conventions upside down, the lady no beauty but dark and treacherous, the loved one beyond considerations of sexual possession because he is male. The sonnet tended to gravitate toward correctness or politeness, and for most readers its chief pleasure must have been rhetorical, in its forceful pleading and consciously exhibited artifice, but, under the pressure of Shakespeare's urgent metaphysical concerns, dramatic toughness, and shifting and highly charged ironies, the form's conventional limits were exploded.

OTHER POETIC STYLES

Sonnet and lyric represent one tradition of verse within the period, that most conventionally delineated as Elizabethan, but the picture is complicated by the coexistence of other poetic styles in which ornament was distrusted or turned to different purposes. The sonnet was even parodied by Sir John Davies in his *Gulling Sonnets* (c. 1594) and by the Jesuit poet Robert Southwell. A particular stimulus to experiment was the variety of new possibilities made available by verse translation, from Richard Stanyhurst's extraordinary *Aeneid* (1582), in quantitative hexameter and littered with obscure or invented diction, and Sir John Harington's version of Ariosto's *Orlando furioso* (1591), with its Byronic ease and narrative fluency, to Christopher Marlowe's blank verse rendering of *Lucan's First Book* (published 1600), probably the finest Elizabethan translation.

The genre to benefit most from translation was the epyllion, or little epic. This short narrative in verse was usually on a mythological subject, taking most of its material from Ovid, either his *Metamorphoses* (English version by Arthur Golding, 1565–67) or his *Heroides* (English version by Turberville, 1567). This form flourished from Lodge's *Scillaes Metamorphosis* (1589) to Francis Beaumont's *Salmacis and Hermaphroditus* (1602) and is best represented by Marlowe's *Hero and Leander* (published 1598) and Shakespeare's *Venus and Adonis* (1593). Ovid's reputation as an esoteric philosopher left its mark on George Chapman's *Ovid's Banquet of Sense* (1595) and Drayton's *Endimion and Phoebe* (1595), in which the love of mortal for goddess becomes a parable of wisdom. But Ovid's real attraction was as an authority on the erotic, and most epyllia treat physical love with sophistication and sympathy, unrelieved by the gloss of allegory—a tendency culminating in John Marston's *The Metamorphosis of Pigmalion's Image* (1598), a poem that has shocked tender sensibilities. Inevitably, the shift of attitude had an effect on style: for Marlowe the experience of translating (inaccurately) Ovid's *Amores* meant a gain for *Hero and Leander* in terms of urbanity and, more important, wit.

With the epyllion comes a hint of the tastes of the following reign, and a similar shift of taste can be felt among those poets of the 1590s who began to modify the ornamental style in the direction of native plainness or Classical restraint. An astute courtier such as Davies might, in his *Orchestra* (1596) and *Hymns of Astraea* (1599), write confident panegyrics to the aging Elizabeth, but in Sir Walter

Raleigh's *Eleventh Book of the Ocean to Cynthia*, a kind of broken pastoral eclogue, praise of the queen is undermined by an obscure but eloquent sense of hopelessness and disillusionment. For Raleigh, the complimental manner seems to be disintegrating under the weight of disgrace and isolation at court. His scattered lyrics—notably "The Lie," a contemptuous dismissal of the court—often draw their resonance from the resources of the plain style. Another courtier whose writing suggests similar pressures is Greville. His *Caelica* (published 1633) begins as a conventional sonnet sequence but gradually abandons Neoplatonism for pessimistic reflections on religion and politics. Other works in his sinewy and demanding verse include philosophical treatises and unperformed melodramas (*Alaham* and *Mustapha*) that have a sombre Calvinist tone, presenting man as a vulnerable creature inhabiting a world of unresolved contradictions:

> *Oh wearisome condition of humanity!*
> *Born under one law, to another bound;*
> *Vainly begot, and yet forbidden vanity,*
> *Created sick, commanded to be sound.*

(*Mustapha*, chorus)

Greville was a friend of Robert Devereux, 2nd earl of Essex, whose revolt against Elizabeth ended in 1601 on the scaffold, and other poets on the edge of the Essex circle fueled the taste for aristocratic heroism and individualist ethics. Chapman's masterpiece, his translation of Homer (1598), is dedicated to Essex, and his original poems are intellectual and recondite, often deliberately difficult and obscure. His abstruseness is a means of restricting his audience to a worthy, understanding elite. Daniel, in his verse *Epistles* (1603) written to various noblemen, strikes a mean between plainness and compliment. His *Musophilus* (1599), dedicated to Greville, defends the worth of poetry but says there are too many frivolous wits writing. The cast of Daniel's mind is stoical, and his language is classically precise. His major project was a verse history of *The Civil Wars Between the Two Houses of Lancaster and York* (1595–1609), and versified history is also strongly represented in Drayton's *Legends* (1593–1607), *Barons' Wars* (1596, 1603), and *England's Heroical Epistles* (1597).

The form that really set its face against Elizabethan politeness was the satire. Satire was related to the complaint, of which there were notable examples by Daniel (*The Complaint of Rosamond*, 1592) and Shakespeare (*The Rape of Lucrece*, 1594) that are dignified and tragic laments in supple verse. But the Elizabethans mistakenly held the term *satire* to derive from the Greek satyros, a satyr, and so set out to match their manner to their matter and make their verses snarl. In the works of the principal satirists, Donne (five satires, 1593–98), Joseph Hall (*Virgidemiarum*, 1597–98), and Marston (*Certain Satires* and *The Scourge of Villainy*, 1598), the denunciation of vice and folly repeatedly tips into invective, raillery, and sheer abuse. The versification of Donne's satires is frequently so rough as barely to be verse at all. Hall apologized for not being harsh enough, and Marston was himself pilloried in Jonson's play *Poetaster* (1601) for using ridiculously difficult language. "Vex all the world," wrote Marston to himself, "so that thyself be pleased." The satirists popularized a new persona, that of the malcontent who denounces his society not from above but from within. Their continuing attraction resides in their self-contradictory delight in the world they profess to abhor and their evident fascination with the minutiae of life in court and city. They were enthusiastically followed by Everard Guilpin, Samuel Rowlands, Thomas Middleton, and Cyril Tourneur, and so

scandalous was the flood of satires that in 1599 their printing was banned. Thereafter the form survived in Jonson's
classically balanced epigrams and poems of the good life,
but its more immediate impact was on the drama, in help-
ing to create the vigorously skeptical voices that people
The Revenger's Tragedy (1607) and Shakespeare's *Hamlet* (*c.*
1599–1601).

PROSE STYLES, 1550–1600

Prose was easily the principal medium in the Elizabethan
period, and, despite the mid-century uncertainties over
the language's weaknesses and strengths—whether coined
and imported words should be admitted; whether the
structural modeling of English prose on Latin writing was
beneficial or, as Bacon would complain, a pursuit of "choice-
ness of phrase" at the expense of "soundness of
argument"—the general attainment of prose writing was
uniformly high, as is often manifested in contexts not conventionally imaginative or "literary," such as tracts,
pamphlets, and treatises. The obvious instance of such
casual success is Richard Hakluyt's *Principal Navigations,
Voyages, and Discoveries of the English Nation* (1589; expanded
1598–1600), a massive collection of travelers' tales, of
which some are highly accomplished narratives. William
Harrison's gossipy, entertaining *Description of England*
(1577), Philip Stubbes's excitable and humane social cri-
tique *The Anatomy of Abuses* (1583), Reginald Scot's anecdotal
Discovery of Witchcraft (1584), and John Stow's invaluable
Survey of London (1598) also deserve passing mention.
William Kempe's account of his morris dance from London
to Norwich, *Kempe's Nine Days' Wonder* (1600), exemplifies a
smaller genre, the newsbook (a type of pamphlet).
    The writers listed above all use an unpretentious style
enlivened with a vivid vocabulary. The early prose fiction,

on the other hand, delights in ingenious formal embellishment at the expense of narrative economy. This runs up against preferences ingrained in the modern reader by the novel, but Elizabethan fiction is not at all novelistic and finds room for debate, song, and the conscious elaboration of style. The unique exception is Gascoigne's *Adventures of Master F.J.* (1573), a tale of thwarted love set in an English great house, which is the first success in English imaginative prose. Gascoigne's story has a surprising authenticity and almost psychological realism (it may be autobiographical), but even so it is heavily imbued with the influence of Castiglione.

The existence of an audience for polite fiction was signaled in the collections of stories imported from France and Italy by William Painter (1566), Geoffrey Fenton (1577), and George Pettie (1576). Pettie, who claimed not to care "to displease twenty men to please one woman," believed his readership was substantially female. There were later collections by Barnaby Rich (1581) and George Whetstone (1583). Historically, their importance was as sources of plots for many Elizabethan plays. The direction fiction was to take was established by John Lyly's *Euphues: The Anatomy of Wit* (1578), which, with its sequel *Euphues and His England* (1580), set a fashion for an extreme rhetorical mannerism that came to be known as euphuism. The plot of Euphues—a rake's fall from virtue and his recovery—is but an excuse for a series of debates, letters, and speechifyings, thick with assonance, antithesis, parallelism, and balance and displaying a pseudoscientific learning. Lyly's style would be successful on the stage, but in fiction its density and monotony are wearying. The other major prose work of the 1570s, Sidney's *Arcadia*, is no less rhetorical (Abraham Fraunce illustrated his handbook of style *The Arcadian Rhetoric* [1588] almost entirely with examples from the *Arcadia*), but with Sidney rhetoric is in the service of psychological insight and an exciting plot. Dozens of imitations of *Arcadia* and *Euphues* followed from the pens of Greene, Lodge, Anthony Munday, Emanuel Forde, and others. None has much distinction.

Prose was to be decisively transformed through its involvement in the bitter and learned controversies of the 1570s and '80s over the reform of the English Church and the problems the controversies raised in matters of authority, obedience, and conscience. The fragile ecclesiastical compromise threatened to collapse under the demands for further reformation made by Elizabeth's more godly subjects, and its defense culminated in Richard Hooker's *Of the Laws of Ecclesiastical Polity* (eight books, 1593–1662), the first English classic of serious prose. Hooker's is a monumental work, structured in massive and complex paragraphs brilliantly re-creating the orotund style of Cicero. His air of maturity and detachment has recommended him to modern tastes, but no more than his opponents was he above the cut and thrust of controversy. On the contrary, his magisterial rhetoric was designed all the more effectively to fix blame onto his enemies, and even his account (in Books VI–VIII) of the relationship of church and state was deemed too sensitive for publication in the 1590s.

More decisive for English fiction was the appearance of the "Martin Marprelate" tracts of 1588–90. These seven pamphlets argued the Puritan case but with an un-Puritanical scurrility and created great scandal by hurling invective and abuse at Elizabeth's bishops with comical gusto. The bishops employed Lyly and Nashe to reply to the pseudonymous Marprelate and the consequence may be read in Nashe's prose satires of the following decade, especially *Piers Penniless His Supplication to the Devil* (1592), *The Unfortunate Traveller* (1594), and Nashe's *Lenten Stuff* (1599), the latter a pamphlet in praise of herring. Nashe's "extemporal vein" makes fullest use of the flexibility of colloquial speech and delights in nonsense, redundancy, and disconcerting shifts of tone, which demand an answering agility from the reader. His language is probably the most profusely inventive of all Elizabethan writers', and he makes even Greene's low-life pamphlets (1591–92), with their sensational tales from the underworld, look conventional. His only rival is Thomas Deloney, whose *Jack of Newbury* (1597), *The Gentle Craft* (1597–98), and *Thomas of Reading* (1600) are enduringly attractive for their depiction of the lives of ordinary citizens, interspersed with elements of romance, jest book, and folktale. Deloney's entirely convincing dialogue indicates how important for the development of a flexible prose must have been the example of a flourishing theatre in Elizabethan London. In this respect, as in so many others, the role of the drama was crucial.

EARLY STUART POETRY AND PROSE

In the early Stuart period the failure of consensus was dramatically demonstrated in the political collapse of the 1640s and in the growing sociocultural divergences of the immediately preceding years. While it was still possible for the theatres to address the nation very much as a single audience, the court—with the Baroque style, derived from the Continent, that it encouraged in painting, masque, and panegyric—was becoming more remote from the country at large and was regarded with increasing distrust. In fact, a growing separation between polite and vulgar literature was to dispel many of the characteristic strengths of Elizabethan writing.

Simultaneously, long-term intellectual changes were beginning to impinge on the status of poetry and prose. Sidney's defense of poetry, which maintained that poetry depicted what was ideally rather than actually true, was rendered redundant by the loss of agreement over transcendent absolutes; the scientist, the Puritan with his inner light, and the skeptic differed equally over the criteria by which truth was to be established. From the circle of Lucius Cary, Viscount Falkland, at Great Tew in Oxfordshire—which included poets such as Edmund Waller, Thomas Carew, and Sidney Godolphin—William Chillingworth argued that it was unreasonable for any individual to force his opinions onto any other, while Thomas Hobbes reached the opposite conclusion (in his *Leviathan,* 1651) that all must be as the state pleases.

In this context, the old idea of poetry as a persuader to virtue fell obsolete, and the century as a whole witnessed a massive transfer of energy into new literary forms, particularly into the rationally balanced couplet, the autobiography, and the embryonic novel. At the same time, these influences were neither uniform nor consistent. Hobbes might repudiate the use of metaphor as senseless and ambiguous, yet his own prose was frequently enlivened by half-submerged metaphors.

House of Stuart

The House of Stuart was the royal house of Scotland from 1371 and of England from 1603. It was interrupted in 1649 by the establishment of the Commonwealth but was restored in 1660. It ended in 1714, when the British crown passed to the house of Hanover.

The first spelling of the family name was undoubtedly Stewart, the old Scots version, but during the 16th century French influence led to the adoption of the spellings Stuart and Steuart, because of the absence of the letter "w" in the French alphabet.

The family can be traced back to 11th-century Brittany, where for at least four generations they were stewards to the counts of Dol. In the early 12th century they appeared in England, and Walter, third son of the 4th steward of Dol, entered the service of David I, king of Scots, and was later appointed his steward, an office that was confirmed to his family by King Malcolm IV in 1157. Walter (d. 1326), the 6th steward, married Marjory, daughter of King Robert I the Bruce, in 1315, and in 1371 their son Robert, as King Robert II, became the first Stewart king of Scotland. The royal Stewarts had an unlucky history, dogged by sudden death, and seven succeeded to the throne as minors.

The direct male line terminated with the death of James V in 1542. His daughter Mary, Queen of Scots (d. 1587), was succeeded in 1567 by her only son (by Henry Stuart, Lord Darnley), James VI.

In 1603 James VI, through his great-grandmother Margaret Tudor, daughter of Henry VII of England, inherited the English throne as King James I. After the execution (1649) of James's son Charles I, the Stuarts were excluded from the throne until the restoration of Charles II in 1660. Charles II was succeeded in 1685 by his Roman Catholic brother James II (d. 1701), who so alienated the sympathies of his subjects that in 1688 William, Prince of Orange, was invited to come "to the rescue of the laws and religion of England." James fled, and by the Bill of Rights (1689) and the Act of Settlement (1701), which denied the crown to any Roman Catholic, he and his descendants were excluded from the throne.

But Stuarts still ruled in England and Scotland, for William was the son of Charles II's sister Mary, and his wife Mary was James II's elder daughter. They became joint sovereigns as William III and Mary II. They left no issue, and the Act of Settlement secured the succession to Mary's sister Anne (d. 1714) and on her death without issue to Sophia, electress of Hanover, a granddaughter of James I. Sophia's son and heir became George I, first of the British House of Hanover.

The last male Stuarts of the British royal line were James II's son James Edward (d. 1766), the Old Pretender, and his sons Charles Edward (d. 1788), the Young Pretender (known as Bonnie Prince Charlie), who died without legitimate issue, and Henry (d. 1807), Cardinal Duke of York.

THE METAPHYSICAL POETS

Writers responded to these conditions in different ways, and in poetry three main traditions may broadly be distinguished, which have been coupled with the names of Edmund Spenser, Ben Jonson, and John Donne. Donne heads the tradition that 18th-century critic Samuel Johnson labeled for all time as the Metaphysicals. What unites these poets as a group is less the violent yoking of unlike ideas to which Johnson objected than that they were all poets of personal and individual feeling, responding to their time's pressures privately or introspectively. This privateness, of course, was not new, but the period in general experienced a huge upsurge of contemplative or devotional verse.

The Metaphysicals

John Donne and other poets of 17th-century England who are noted for the personal, intellectual complexity and concentration that is displayed in their poetry are generally known as the Metaphysicals. Donne is considered the most important of these poets. Others include Henry Vaughan, Andrew Marvell, John Cleveland, and Abraham Cowley as well as, to a lesser extent, George Herbert and Richard Crashaw.

Their work is a blend of emotion and intellectual ingenuity, characterized by conceit or "wit"—that is, by the sometimes violent yoking together of apparently unconnected ideas and things so that the reader is startled out of his complacency and forced to think through the argument of the poem. Metaphysical poetry is less concerned with expressing feeling than with analyzing it, with the poet exploring the recesses of his consciousness. The boldness of the literary devices used—

especially obliquity, irony, and paradox—are often reinforced by a dramatic directness of language and by rhythms derived from that of living speech.

Esteem for Metaphysical poetry never stood higher than in the 1930s and '40s, largely because of T.S. Eliot's influential essay "The Metaphysical Poets" (1921), a review of Herbert J.C. Grierson's anthology *Metaphysical Lyrics & Poems of the Seventeenth Century*. In this essay Eliot argued that the works of these men embody a fusion of thought and feeling that later poets were unable to achieve because of a "dissociation of sensibility," which resulted in works that were either intellectual or emotional but not both at once.

In their own time, however, the epithet *metaphysical* was used pejoratively. In 1630 the Scottish poet William Drummond of Hawthornden objected to those of his contemporaries who attempted to "abstract poetry to metaphysical ideas and scholastic quiddities." At the end of the century John Dryden censured Donne for affecting "the metaphysics" and for perplexing "the minds of the fair sex with nice speculations of philosophy when he should engage their hearts with the softnesses of love." Samuel Johnson, in referring to the learning that their poetry displays, also dubbed them "the metaphysical poets," and the term has continued in use ever since. Eliot's adoption of the label as a term of praise is arguably a better guide to his personal aspirations about his own poetry than to the Metaphysical poets themselves. His use of *metaphysical* underestimates these poets' debt to lyrical and socially engaged verse. Nonetheless, the term is useful for identifying the often-intellectual character of their writing.

JOHN DONNE

Donne has been taken to be the apex of the 16th-century tradition of plain poetry, and certainly the love lyrics of his that parade their cynicism, indifference, and libertinism pointedly invert and parody the conventions of Petrarchan lyric, though he courts admiration for his poetic virtuosity no less than the Petrarchans. A "great haunter of plays" in his youth, he is always dramatic. His verse cultivates "strong lines," dissonance, and colloquiality. Carew praised him for avoiding poetic myths and excluding from his verse the "train of gods and goddesses". What fills it instead is a dazzling battery of language and argument drawn from science, law and trade, court and city.

Donne is the first London poet: his early satires and elegies are packed with the busy metropolitan milieu, and his songs and sonnets, which include his best writing, with their kaleidoscope of contradictory attitudes, ironies, and contingencies, explore the alienation and ennui of urban living. He treats experience as relative, a matter of individual point of view. The personality is multiple, quizzical, and inconsistent, eluding definition. His love poetry is that of the frustrated careerist. By inverting normal perspectives and making the mistress the centre of his being—he boasts that she is "all states, and all princes, I, nothing else is"—he belittles the public world, defiantly asserting the superior validity of his private experience, and frequently he erodes the traditional dichotomy of body and soul, outrageously praising the mistress in language reserved for platonic or religious contexts. The defiance is complicated, however, by a recurrent conviction of personal unworthiness that culminates in the *Anniversaries* (1611–12), two long commemorative poems written on the death of a patron's daughter. These expand into the classic statement of Jacobean melancholy, an intense meditation on the vanity of the world and the collapse of traditional certainties. Donne would, reluctantly, find respectability in a church career, but even his religious poems are torn between the same tense self-assertion and self-abasement that mark his secular poetry.

Among the leading Metaphysical poets, John Donne was lauded by many and derided by others for his "plain" verse and use of strong, dramatic language. Hulton Archive/Getty Images

DONNE'S INFLUENCE

Donne's influence was vast. The taste for wit and conceits reemerged in dozens of minor lyricists, among them courtiers such as Aurelian Townshend and William Habington, academics such as William Cartwright, and religious poets such as Francis Quarles and Henry King. The only true Metaphysical, in the sense of a poet with genuinely philosophical pretensions, was Edward Herbert (Lord Herbert of Cherbury), important as an early proponent of religion formulated by the light of reason.

Donne's most enduring followers were the three major religious poets George Herbert, Richard Crashaw, and Henry Vaughan. Herbert, a Cambridge academic who buried his courtly ambitions in the quiet life of a country parsonage, wrote some of the most resonant and attractive religious verse in the language. Though not devoid of tension, his poems substitute for Donne's tortured selfhood a humane, meditative assurance. They evoke a practical piety and a richly domestic world, but they dignify it with a musicality and a feeling for the beauty of holiness that bespeak Herbert's identification with the nascent Anglican church of Archbishop William Laud. By contrast, the poems of Crashaw (a Roman Catholic) and the Welsh recluse Vaughan move in alternative traditions: the former toward the sensuous ecstasies and effusions of the Continental Baroque, the latter toward hermetic naturalism and mystical raptures.

However, in the context of the Civil Wars, Vaughan's and Crashaw's introspection began to look like retreat, and, when the satires of John Cleveland and the lyrics of Abraham Cowley took the Donne manner to extremes of paradox and vehemence, it was symptomatic of a loss of control in the face of political and social traumas. The one poet for whom metaphysical wit became a strategy for holding together conflicting allegiances was Donne's outstanding heir, Andrew Marvell. Marvell's writing is taut, extraordinarily dense and precise, uniquely combining a cavalier lyric grace with Puritanical economy of statement. His finest work seems to have been done at the time of greatest strain, in about 1650–53, and under the patronage of Sir Thomas Fairfax, parliamentarian general but opponent of King Charles I's execution, to whose retirement from politics to his country estate Marvell accorded qualified praise in "Upon Appleton House".

Marvell's lyrics are poems of the divided mind, sensitive to all the major conflicts of their society—body against soul, action against retirement, experience against innocence, Oliver Cromwell against the king—but he sustains the conflict of irreconcilables through paradox and wit rather than attempting to decide or transcend it. In this situation, irresolution has become a strength. In a poem like "An Horatian Ode upon Cromwell's Return from Ireland," which weighs the claims of King Charles and Cromwell, the poet's reserve was the only effective way of confronting the unprecedented demise of traditional structures of politics and morality.

BEN JONSON AND THE CAVALIER POETS

In contrast to Donne stood the writing of Ben Jonson. The Jonsonian tradition was, broadly, that of social verse, written with a Classical clarity and weight and deeply informed by ideals of civilized reasonableness, ceremonious respect, and inner self-sufficiency derived from Seneca. It is a poetry of publicly shared values and norms. Ben Jonson's own verse was occasional. It addresses other individuals, distributes praise and blame, and promulgates sober and judicious ethical attitudes. His favoured forms were the ode, elegy, satire, epistle, and epigram, and they are always beautifully crafted objects, achieving a Classical symmetry and monumentality. For Jonson, the unornamented style meant not colloquiality but labour, restraint, and control. A good poet had first to be a good man, and his verses lead his society toward an ethic of gracious but responsible living.

With the Cavalier poets who succeeded Jonson, the element of urbanity and conviviality tended to loom larger. Robert Herrick was perhaps England's first poet to express impatience with the tediousness of country life. However, Herrick's "The Country Life" and "The Hock Cart" rival Jonson's To Penshurst as panegyrics to the Horatian ideal of the "good life," calm and retired, but Herrick's poems gain retrospective poignancy by their implied contrast with the disruptions of the Civil Wars. The courtiers Carew, Sir John Suckling, and Richard Lovelace developed a manner of ease and naturalness suitable to the world of gentlemanly pleasure in which they moved. Suckling's A *Session of the Poets* (1637; published 1646) lists more than 20 wits then in town.

The Cavalier poets were writing England's first vers de société, lyrics of compliments and casual liaisons, often cynical, occasionally obscene. This was a line to be picked up again after 1660, as were the heroic verse and attitudinizing drama of Jonson's successor as poet laureate, Sir William Davenant. A different contribution was the elegance and smoothness that came to be associated with Sir John Denham and Edmund Waller, whom the poet John Dryden named as the first exponents of "good writing." Waller's inoffensive lyrics are the epitome of polite taste, and Denham's topographical poem "Cooper's Hill" (1641), a significant work in its own right, is an important precursor of the balanced Augustan couplet (as is the otherwise slight oeuvre of Viscount

Falkland). The growth of Augustan gentility was further encouraged by work done on translations in mid-century,particularly by Sir Richard Fanshawe and Thomas Stanley.

CONTINUED INFLUENCE OF SPENSER

Donne had shattered Edmund Spenser's leisurely orna-mentation, and Jonson censured his archaic language, but the continuing regard for Spenser at this time was significant. Variants of the Spenserian stanza were used by the brothers Giles Fletcher and Phineas Fletcher, the former in his long religious poem Christ's Victory (1610), which is also indebted to Josuah Sylvester's highly popular translations from the French Calvinist poet Guillaume du Bartas, the *Divine Weeks and Works* (1605). Similarly, Spenserian pastorals still flowed from the pens of William Browne (*Britannia's Pastorals*, 1613–16), George Wither (*The Shepherd's Hunting*, 1614), and Michael Drayton, who at the end of his life returned nostalgically to portraying an idealized Elizabethan golden age (*The Muses Elizium*, 1630).

Nostalgia was a dangerous quality under the progressive and absolutist Stuarts. The taste for Spenser involved a respect for values—traditional, patriotic, and Protestant—that were popularly, if erroneously, linked with the Elizabethan past but thought to be disregarded by the new regime. These poets believed they had a spokesman at court in the heroic and promising Prince Henry, but his death in 1612 disappointed many expectations, intellectual, political, and religious, and this group in particular was forced further toward the Puritan position. Increasingly, their pastorals and fervently Protestant poetry made them seem out of step with a court whose sympathies in foreign affairs were pro-Spanish and pro-Catholic. So sharp became Wither's satires that he earned imprisonment and was lampooned by Jonson in a court masque. The failure of the Stuarts to conciliate attitudes such as these was to be crucial to their inability to prevent the collapse of the Elizabethan compromise in the next generation. The nearest affinities, both in style and substance, of John Milton's early poetry would be with the Spenserians. In *Areopagitica* (1644) Milton praised "our sage and serious poet Spenser" as "a better teacher than [the philosophers] Scotus or Aquinas."

Spenserian Stanza

The Spenserian stanza is a verse form that consists of eight iambic pentameter lines followed by a ninth line of six iambic feet (an alexandrine). The rhyme scheme is *ababbcbcc*. The first eight lines produce an effect of formal unity, while the hexameter completes the thought of the stanza. Invented by Edmund Spenser for his poem *The Faerie Queene* (1590–1609), the Spenserian stanza has origins in the Old French ballade (eight-line stanzas, rhyming *ababbcbc*), the Italian ottava rima (eight iambic pentameter lines with a rhyme scheme of *abababcc*), and the stanza form used by Chaucer in his "Monk's Tale" (eight lines rhyming *ababbcbc*). A revolutionary innovation in its day, the Spenserian stanza fell into general disuse during the 17th and 18th centuries. It was revived in the 19th century by the Romantic poets—e.g., Byron used it in *Childe Harold's Pilgrimage* and Keats in "The Eve of St. Agnes," and Shelley in "Adonais."

THE EFFECT OF RELIGION AND SCIENCE ON EARLY STUART PROSE

Puritanism also had a powerful effect on early Stuart prose. The best sellers of the period were godly manuals that ran to scores of editions, such as Arthur Dent's *Plain Man's Pathway to Heaven* (25 editions by 1640) and Lewis Bayly's Practice of Piety (1611; some 50 editions followed), two copies of which formed the meagre dowry of preacher and author John Bunyan's first wife. Puritans preferred sermons in the plain style too, eschewing rhetoric for an austerely edifying treatment of doctrine, though some famous preachers, such as Henry Smith and Thomas Adams, believed it their duty to make the word of God eloquent. The other factor shaping prose was the desire among scientists for a utilitarian style that would accurately and concretely represent the relationship between words and things, without figurative luxuriance. This hope, repeatedly voiced in the 1640s and '50s, eventually bore fruit in the practice of the Royal Society (founded 1660), which decisively affected prose after the Restoration. Its impact on earlier writing, though, was limited. Most early Stuart science was written in a baroque style.

The impetus toward a scientific prose derived ultimately from Sir Francis Bacon, the towering intellect of the century, who charted a philosophical system well in advance of his generation and beyond his own powers to complete. In the *Advancement of Learning* (1605) and the *Novum Organum* (1620), Bacon visualized a great synthesis of knowledge, rationally and comprehensively ordered so that each discipline might benefit from the discoveries of the others. The two radical novelties of his scheme were his insight that there could be progress in learning (i.e., that the limits of knowledge were not fixed but could be pushed forward) and his inductive method, which aimed to establish scientific principles by experimentation, beginning at particulars and working toward generalities, instead of working backward from preconceived systems.

Bacon democratized knowledge at a stroke, removing the tyranny of authority and lifting scientific inquiry free of religion and ethics and into the domain of mechanically operating second causes (though he held that the perfection of the machine itself testified to God's glory). The implications for prose are contained in his statement in the *Advancement* that the preoccupation with words instead of matter was the first "distemper" of learning. His own prose, however, was far from plain. The level exposition of idea in the *Advancement* is underpinned by a tactful but firmly persuasive rhetoric, and the famous *Essays* (1597; enlarged 1612, 1625) are shifting and elusive, teasing the reader toward unresolved contradictions and half-apprehended complications.

The *Essays* are masterworks in the new Stuart genre of the prose of leisure, the reflectively aphoristic prose piece in imitation of the Essays of Michel de Montaigne. Lesser collections were published by Sir William Cornwallis (1600–01), Owen Felltham (1623), and Ben Jonson (*Timber; or, Discoveries*, published posthumously in 1640). A related genre was the "character," a brief, witty description of a social or moral type, imitated from Theophrastus and practiced first by Joseph Hall (*Characters of Virtues and Vices*, 1608) and later by Sir Thomas Overbury, John Webster, and Thomas Dekker. The best characters are John Earle's (*Micro-cosmography*, 1628). Character-writing led naturally into the writing of biography. The chief practitioners of this genre were Thomas Fuller, who included brief sketches in *The Holy State* (1642; includes *The Profane State*), and Izaak Walton, the biographer of Donne, George Herbert, and Richard Hooker. Walton's biographies are entertaining, but he manipulated facts shamelessly. These texts seem lightweight when placed beside Fulke Greville's tragic and valedictory *Life of the Renowned Sir Philip Sidney* (*c.* 1610; published 1652).

The major historical work of the period was Sir Walter Raleigh's unfinished *History of the World* (1614), with its rolling sentences and sombre skepticism, written from the Tower of London during his disgrace. Raleigh's providential framework would recommend his *History* to Cromwell and Milton. King James I found it "too saucy in censuring princes." Bacon's *History of the Reign of King Henry the Seventh* (1622) belongs to a more secular, Machiavellian tradition, which valued history for its lessons in pragmatism.

PROSE STYLES

The essayists and character writers initiated a reaction against the orotund flow of serious Elizabethan prose that has been variously described as metaphysical, anti-Ciceronian, or Senecan, but these terms are used vaguely to denote both the cultivation of a clipped, aphoristic prose style, curt to the point of obscurity, and a fashion for looseness, asymmetry, and open-endedness. The age's professional stylists were the preachers, and in the sermons of Donne and Lancelot Andrewes the clipped style is used to crumble the preacher's exegesis into tiny, hopping fragments or to suggest a nervous, agitated restlessness.

An extreme example of the loose style is Robert Burton's *Anatomy of Melancholy* (1621), a massive encyclopaedia of learning, pseudoscience, and anecdote strung around an investigation into human psychopathology. Burton's compendiousness, his fascination with excess, necessitated a style that was infinitely extensible. His successor was Sir Thomas Urquhart, whose translation of

François Rabelais's *Gargantua* and *Pantagruel* (1653) out-does even its author in invention. In the *Religio Medici* (1635) and in *The Garden of Cyrus* and *Hydriotaphia, Urn Burial*; or, *A Discourse of the Sepulchral Urns Lately Found in Norfolk* (both printed 1658) of Sir Thomas Browne, the loose style serves a mind delighting in paradox and unan-swerable speculation, content with uncertainty because of its intuitive faith in ultimate assurance. Browne's majestic prose invests his confession of his belief and his antiquar-ian and scientific tracts alike with an almost Byzantine richness and melancholy.

These were all learned styles, Latinate and sophisti-cated, but the appearance in the 1620s of the first corantos, or courants (news books), generated by interest in the Thirty Years' War, heralded the great 17th-century shift from an elite to a mass readership, a change consolidated by the explosion of popular journalism that accompanied the political confusion of the 1640s. The search for new kinds of political order and authority generated an answer-ing chaos of styles, as voices were heard that had hitherto been denied access to print. The radical ideas of educated political theorists like Hobbes and the republican James Harrington were advanced within the traditional decen-cies of polite (if ruthless) debate, but they spoke in competition with writers who deliberately breached the literary canons of good taste. These competitors were Levelers, such as John Lilburne and Richard Overton, with their vigorously dramatic manner; Diggers, such as Gerrard Winstanley in his *Law of Freedom* (1652); and Ranters, whose language and syntax were as disruptive as the libertinism they professed. The outstanding examples are Milton's tracts against the bishops (1641–42), which revealed an unexpected talent for scurrilous abuse and withering sarcasm. Milton's later pamphlets—on divorce, education, and free speech (*Areopagitica*, 1644) and in

defense of tyrannicide *(The Tenure of Kings* and *Magistrates,*
1649)—adopt a loosely Ciceronian sonorousness, but their
language is plain and always intensely imaginative and
absorbing.

JOHN MILTON
AND THE RENAISSANCE

John Milton, the last great poet of the English Renaissance,
laid down in his work the foundations for the emerging
aesthetic of the post-Renaissance period. Milton had a
concept of the public role of the poet even more elevated,
if possible, than Jonson's. He early declared his hope to do
for his native tongue what "the greatest and choicest wits
of Athens, Rome, or modern Italy" had done for theirs.
But where Jonson's humanism had led him into court service, Milton's was complicated by a respect for the
conscience acting in pursuance of those things that it,
individually, knew were right. He wished to "contribute to
the progress of real and substantial liberty; which is to be
sought for not from without, but within." His early verse
aligned him, poetically and politically, with the Spenserians:
religious and pastoral odes; "Lycidas" (1637), a pastoral
elegy that incidentally bewails the state of the church; and
Comus (1634), a masque against "masquing," performed
privately in the country and opposing a private heroism in
chastity and virtue to the courtly round of revelry and
pleasure. But he was also well read in Latin and modern
Italian literature and ambitious to write in English a poem
to compare with Virgil's *Aeneid.*

During the Civil Wars and the Cromwellian republic
(1642–60), Milton saw his role as the intellectual serving
the state in a glorious cause. He devoted his energies to
pamphleteering, first in the cause of church reform and
then in defense of the fledgling republic, and he became

During the English Civil Wars, John Milton was a pamphleteer and author of revolutionary tracts. Social, political, and religious themes permeate his later verse works as well. Hulton Archive/Getty Images

Latin secretary to Cromwell's Council of State. But the republic of virtue failed to materialize, and the Cromwellian settlement was swept aside in 1660 by the returning monarchy. Milton showed himself virtually the last defender of the republic with his tract *The Ready and Easy Way to Establish a Free Commonwealth* (1660), a courageous but desperate program for a permanent oligarchy of the Puritan elect, the only device he could suggest to prevent the return to royal slavery.

Milton's greatest achievements were yet to come, for *Paradise Lost*, *Paradise Regained*, and *Samson Agonistes* were not published until after the Restoration. But their roots were deep in the radical experience of the 1640s and '50s and in the ensuing transformations in politics and society. With its antihero, Satan, in flawed rebellion against an all-powerful divine monarchy, *Paradise Lost* revisits the politics of the last generation. Its all-too-human protagonists, turned out of Eden into a more difficult world where they have to acquire new and less-certain kinds of heroism, are adjusting to a culture in which all the familiar bearings have been changed, the old public certainties now rendered more private, particular, and provisional. For Milton and his contemporaries, 1660 was a watershed that necessitated a complete rethinking of assumptions and a corresponding reassessment of the literary language, traditions, and forms appropriate to the new age.

MILTON'S LIFE AND WORKS

Milton's paternal grandfather, Richard, was a staunch Roman Catholic who expelled his son John, the poet's father, from the family home in Oxfordshire for reading an English (i.e., Protestant) Bible. Banished and disinherited, Milton's father established in London a business as a scrivener, preparing documents for legal transactions. He was also a moneylender, and he negotiated with creditors to arrange for loans on behalf of his clients. He and his wife, Sara Jeffrey, whose father was a merchant tailor, had three children who survived their early years: Anne, the oldest, followed by John and Christopher. Though Christopher became a lawyer, a Royalist, and perhaps a

Roman Catholic, he maintained throughout his life a cordial relationship with his older brother. After the Stuart monarchy was restored in 1660, Christopher, among others, may have interceded to prevent the execution of his brother.

The elder John Milton, who fostered cultural interests as a musician and composer, enrolled his son John at St. Paul's School, probably in 1620, and employed tutors to supplement his son's formal education. Milton was privately tutored by Thomas Young, a Scottish Presbyterian who may have influenced his gifted student in religion and politics while they maintained contact across subsequent decades. At St. Paul's Milton befriended Charles Diodati, a fellow student who would become his confidant through young adulthood. During his early years, Milton may have heard sermons by the poet John Donne, dean of St. Paul's Cathedral, which was within view of his school. Educated in Latin and Greek there, Milton in due course acquired proficiency in other languages, especially Italian, in which he composed some sonnets and which he spoke as proficiently as a native Italian, according to the testimony of Florentines whom he befriended during his travel abroad in 1638–39.

Milton enrolled at Christ's College, Cambridge, in 1625, presumably to be educated for the ministry. A year later he was "rusticated," or temporarily expelled, for a period of time because of a conflict with one of his tutors, the logician William Chappell. He was later reinstated under another tutor, Nathaniel Tovey. In 1629 Milton was awarded a bachelor of arts degree, and in 1632 he received a master of arts degree. Despite his initial intent to enter the ministry, Milton did not do so, a situation that has not been fully explained. Possible reasons are that Milton lacked respect for his fellow students who were planning to become ministers but whom he considered ill-equipped academically or that his Puritan inclinations, which became more radical as he matured, caused him to dislike the hierarchy of the established church and its insistence on uniformity of worship. Perhaps, too, his self-evident disaffection impelled the Church of England to reject him for the ministry.

Overall, Milton was displeased with Cambridge, possibly because study there emphasized Scholasticism, which he found stultifying to the imagination. Moreover, in correspondence with a former tutor at St. Paul's School, Alexander Gill, Milton complained about a lack of friendship with fellow students. They called him the "Lady of Christ's College," perhaps because of his fair complexion, delicate features, and auburn hair. Nonetheless, Milton excelled academically. At Cambridge he composed several academic exercises called prolusions, which were presented as oratorical performances in the manner of a debate. In such exercises, students applied their learning in logic and rhetoric, among other disciplines. Milton authorized publication of seven of his prolusions, composed and recited in Latin, in 1674, the year of his death.

In 1632, after seven years at Cambridge, Milton returned to his family home, now in Hammersmith, on the outskirts of London. Three years later, perhaps because of an outbreak of the plague, the family relocated to a more pastoral setting, Horton, in Buckinghamshire. In these two locations, Milton spent approximately six years in studious retirement, during which he read Greek and Latin authors chiefly. Without gainful employment, Milton was supported by his father during this period.

In 1638, accompanied by a manservant, Milton undertook a tour of the Continent for about 15 months, most of which he spent in Italy, primarily Rome and Florence. The Florentine academies especially appealed to Milton, and he befriended young members of the Italian literati, whose similar humanistic interests he found gratifying. Invigorated by their admiration for him, he corresponded with his Italian friends after his return to England, though he never saw them again. While in Florence, Milton also met with Galileo, who was under virtual house arrest. The circumstances of this extraordinary meeting, whereby a young Englishman about 30 years old gained access to the aged and blind astronomer, are unknown. (Galileo would become the only contemporary whom Milton mentioned by name in *Paradise Lost*.) While in Italy, Milton learned of the death in 1638 of Charles Diodati, his closest boyhood companion from St. Paul's School, possibly a victim of the plague. He also learned of impending civil war in England, news that caused him to return home sooner than anticipated. Back in England, Milton took up residence in London, not far from Bread Street, where he had been born. In his household were John and Edward Phillips— sons of his sister Anne—whom he tutored. Upon his return he composed an elegy in Latin, Epitaphium Damonis ("Damon's Epitaph"), which commemorated Diodati.

Early Poetic and Prose Works

By the time he returned to England in 1639, Milton had manifested remarkable talent as a linguist and translator and extraordinary versatility as a poet. While at St. Paul's, as a 15-year-old student, Milton had translated Psalm 114 from the original Hebrew, a text that recounts the liberation of the Israelites from Egypt. This translation into English was a poetic paraphrase in heroic couplets (rhymed iambic pentameter), and later he translated and paraphrased the same psalm into Greek. Beginning such work early in his boyhood, he continued it into adulthood, especially from 1648 to 1653, a period when he was also composing pamphlets against the Church of England and the monarchy. Also in his early youth Milton composed letters in Latin verse. These letters, which range over many topics, are called elegies because they employ elegiac metre—a verse form, Classical in origin, that consists of couplets, the first line dactylic hexameter, the second dactylic pentameter. Milton's first elegy, "Elegia prima ad Carolum Diodatum, was a letter to Diodati," who was a student at Oxford while Milton attended Cambridge. But Milton's letter was written from London in 1626, during his period of rustication. In the poem he anticipates his reinstatement, when he will "go back to the reedy fens of the Cam and return again to the hum of the noisy school."

Another early poem in Latin is "In Quintum Novembris" ("On the Fifth of November"), which Milton composed in 1626 at Cambridge. The poem celebrates the anniversary of the failed Gunpowder Plot of 1605, when Guy Fawkes was discovered preparing to detonate explosives at the opening of Parliament, an event in which King James I and his family would participate. On the event's anniversary, university students typically composed poems that attacked Roman Catholics for their involvement in treachery of this kind. The papacy and the Catholic nations on the Continent also came under attack. Milton's poem includes two larger themes that would later inform *Paradise Lost*: that the evil perpetrated by sinful humankind may be counteracted by Providence and that God will bring greater goodness out of evil. Throughout his career, Milton inveighed against Catholicism, though during his travels in Italy in 1638–39 he developed cordial personal relationships with Catholics, including high-ranking officials who oversaw the library at the Vatican.

In 1628 Milton composed an occasional poem, "On the Death of a Fair Infant Dying of a Cough," which mourns the loss of his niece Anne, the daughter of his older sister. Milton tenderly commemorates the child, who was two years old. The poem's conceits, Classical allusions, and theological overtones emphasize that the child entered the supernal realm because the human condition, having been enlightened by her brief presence, was ill-suited to bear her any longer.

In this early period, Milton's principal poems included "On the Morning of Christ's Nativity," "On Shakespeare," and the so-called companion poems "L'Allegro" and "Il Penseroso". Milton's sixth elegy (*Elegia sexta*), a verse letter in Latin sent to Diodati in December 1629, provides valuable insight into his conception of On the Morning of Christ's Nativity. Informing Diodati of his literary activity, Milton recounts that he is

> *singing the heaven-descended King, the bringer of peace, and the blessed times promised in the sacred books—the infant cries of our God and his stabling under a mean roof who, with his Father, governs the realms above.*

The advent of the Christ child, he continues, results in the pagan gods being "destroyed in their own shrines." In effect, Milton likens Christ to the source of light that, by dispelling the darkness of paganism, initiates the onset of Christianity and silences the pagan oracles. Milton's summary in the sixth elegy makes clear his central argument in "On the Morning of Christ's Nativity": that the Godhead's descent and humiliation is crucial to the Christ child's triumph. Through this exercise of humility, the Godhead on behalf of humankind becomes victorious over the powers of death and darkness.

"On Shakespeare," though composed in 1630, first appeared anonymously as one of the many encomiums in the Second Folio (1632) of Shakespeare's plays. It was Milton's first published poem in English. In the 16-line epigram Milton contends that no man-made monument is a suitable tribute to Shakespeare's achievement. According to Milton, Shakespeare himself created the most enduring monument to befit his genius: the readers of the plays, who, transfixed with awe and wonder, become living monuments, a process renewed at each generation through the panorama of time. "L'Allegro" and "Il Penseroso," written about 1631, may reflect the dialectic that informed the prolusions that Milton composed at Cambridge. The former celebrates the activities of daytime, and the latter muses on the sights, sounds, and emotions associated with darkness. The former describes a lively and sanguine personality, whereas the latter dwells on a pensive, even melancholic, temperament. In their complementary interaction, the poems may dramatize how a wholesome personality blends aspects of mirth and melancholy. Some commentators suggest that Milton may be allegorically portraying his own personality in "Il Penseroso" and Diodati's more outgoing and carefree disposition in "L'Allegro". If such is the case, then in their friendship Diodati provided the balance that offset Milton's marked temperament of studious retirement.

Milton's most important early poems, *Comus* and "Lycidas," are major literary achievements, to the extent that his reputation as an author would have been secure by 1640 even without his later works. *Comus*, a dramatic entertainment, or masque, is also called *A Mask*. It was first published as *A Maske Presented at Ludlow Castle* in 1638, but, since the late 17th century, it has typically been called by the name of its most vivid character, the villainous Comus. Performed in 1634 on "Michaelmas" (September 29) at Ludlow Castle in Shropshire, *Comus* celebrates the installation of John Egerton, earl of Bridgewater and Viscount Brackley and a member of Charles I's Privy Council, as lord president of Wales. In addition to various English and Welsh dignitaries, the installation was attended by Egerton's wife and children. The latter—Alice (15 years old), John (11), and Thomas (9)—all had parts in the dramatic entertainment. Other characters include Thyrsis, an attendant spirit to the children; Sabrina, a nymph of the River Severn; and Comus, a necromancer and seducer. Henry Lawes, who played the part of Thyrsis, was a musician and composer, the music teacher of the Egerton children, and the composer of the music for the songs of *Comus*. Presumably Lawes invited Milton to write the masque, which not only consists of songs and dialogue but also features dances, scenery, and stage properties.

The masque develops the theme of a journey through the woods by the three Egerton children, in the course of which the daughter, called "the Lady," is separated from her brothers. While alone, she encounters Comus, who is disguised as a villager and who claims that he will lead her to her brothers. Deceived by his amiable countenance, the Lady follows him, only to be victimized by his necromancy. Seated on an enchanted chair, she is immobilized, and Comus accosts her while with one hand he holds a necromancer's wand and with the other he offers a vessel with a drink that would overpower her. Within view at his palace is an array of cuisine intended to arouse the Lady's appetites and desires.

Despite being restrained against her will, she continues to exercise right reason (*recta ratio*) in her disputation with Comus, thereby manifesting her freedom of mind. Whereas the would-be seducer argues that appetites and desires issuing from one's nature are "natural" and therefore licit, the Lady contends that only rational self-control is enlightened and virtuous. To be self-indulgent and intemperate, she adds, is to forfeit one's higher nature and to yield to baser impulses. In this debate the Lady and Comus signify, respectively, soul and body, ratio and libido,

sublimation and sensualism, virtue and vice, moral rectitude and immoral depravity.

In line with the theme of the journey that distinguishes
Comus, the Lady has been deceived by the guile of a
treacherous character, temporarily waylaid, and besieged
by sophistry that is disguised as wisdom. As she continues
to assert her freedom of mind and to exercise her free will
by resistance, even defiance, she is rescued by the attendant spirit and her brothers. Ultimately, she and her
brothers are reunited with their parents in a triumphal
celebration, which signifies the heavenly bliss awaiting
the wayfaring soul that prevails over trials and travails,
whether these are the threats posed by overt evil or the
blandishments of temptation.

Late in 1637 Milton composed a pastoral elegy called
"Lycidas," which commemorates the death of a fellow student at Cambridge, Edward King, who drowned while
crossing the Irish Sea. Published in 1638 in *Justa Edouardo
King Naufrago* ("Obsequies in Memory of Edward King"),
a compilation of elegies by Cambridge students, "Lycidas"
is one of several poems in English, whereas most of the
others are in Greek and Latin. As a pastoral elegy—often
considered the most outstanding example of the genre—
Milton's poem is richly allegorical. King is called Lycidas,
a shepherd's name that recurs in Classical elegies. By
choosing this name, Milton signals his participation in the
tradition of memorializing a loved one through pastoral
poetry, a practice that may be traced from ancient Greek
Sicily through Roman culture and into the Christian
Middle Ages and early Renaissance.

The poem's speaker, a persona for Milton's own voice,
is a fellow shepherd who mourns the loss of a friend with
whom he shared duties in tending sheep. The pastoral
allegory of the poem conveys that King and Milton were

colleagues whose studious interests and academic activities were similar. In the course of commemorating King, the speaker challenges divine justice obliquely. Through allegory, the speaker accuses God of unjustly punishing the young, selfless King, whose premature death ended a career that would have unfolded in stark contrast to the majority of the ministers and bishops of the Church of England, whom the speaker condemns as depraved, materialistic, and selfish.

Informing the poem is satire of the episcopacy and ministry, which Milton heightens through invective and the use of odious metaphors, thereby anticipating his later diatribes against the Church of England in the antiprelatical tracts of the 1640s. Likening bishops to vermin infesting sheep and consuming their innards, Milton depicts the prelates in stark contrast to the ideal of the Good Shepherd that is recounted in the Gospel according to John. In this context, the speaker weighs the worldly success of the prelates and ministers against King's death by drowning. The imagery of the poem depicts King being resurrected in a process of lustration from the waters in which he was immersed. Burnished by the sun's rays at dawn, King resplendently ascends heavenward to his eternal reward. The prelates and ministers, though prospering on earth, will encounter St. Peter in the afterlife, who will smite them in an act of retributive justice. Though Milton dwells on King's vocation as a minister, he also acknowledges that his Cambridge colleague was a poet whose death prevented him from establishing a literary reputation. Many commentators suggest that, in King, Milton created an alter ego, with King's premature death reminding Milton that the vicissitudes of fate can interrupt long-standing aspirations and deny the fulfillment of one's talents, whether ministerial or poetic.

REVOLUTIONARY TRACTS

Having returned from abroad in 1639, Milton turned his attention from poetry to prose. In doing so, he entered the controversies surrounding the abolition of the Church of England and of the Royalist government, at times replying to, and often attacking vehemently, English and Continental polemicists who targeted him as the apologist of radical religious and political dissent. In 1641–42 Milton composed five tracts on the reformation of church government. One of these tracts, *Of Reformation*, examines the historical changes in the Church of England since its inception under King Henry VIII and criticizes the continuing resemblances between the Church of England and the Roman Catholic Church, especially the hierarchy in ecclesiastical government. In this tract and others, Milton also calls attention to resemblances between the ecclesiastical and political hierarchies in England, suggesting that the monarchical civil government influences the similar structure of the church. He likewise decries the unduly complicated arguments of theologians, whereas he praises the simplicity and clarity of Scripture.

In another tract from this period, *The Reason of Church Government*, Milton appears to endorse Scottish Presbyterianism as a replacement for the episcopal hierarchy of the Church of England. A few years thereafter, he came to realize that Presbyterianism could be as inflexible as the Church of England in matters of theology, and he became more independent from established religion of all kinds, arguing for the primacy of Scripture and for the conscience of each believer as the guide to interpretation. In another tract from the period 1641–42, *An Apology Against a Pamphlet*, Milton verges on autobiography as he refutes scurrilous allegations attributed to Bishop Joseph Hall.

Soon after these controversies, Milton became embroiled in another conflict, one in his domestic life. Having married Mary Powell in 1642, Milton was a few months afterward deserted by his wife, who returned to her family's residence in Oxfordshire. The reason for their separation is unknown, though perhaps Mary adhered to the Royalist inclinations of her family whereas her husband was progressively anti-Royalist. Or perhaps the discrepancy in their ages—he was 34, she was 17—led to a lack of mutual understanding. During her absence of approximately three years, Milton may have been planning marriage to another woman. But after Mary's return, she and Milton evidently overcame the causes of their estrangement. Three daughters (Anne, Mary, and Deborah) were born, but a son, John, died at age one. Milton's wife died in 1652 after giving birth to Deborah.

During his domestic strife and after his wife's desertion, Milton probably began to frame the arguments of four prose tracts: *The Doctrine and Discipline of Divorce* (1643, enlarged 2nd ed. 1644), *The Judgment of Martin Bucer Concerning Divorce* (1644), *Tetrachordon* (1645), and *Colasterion* (1645). Whether or not his personal experience with Mary affected his views on marriage, Milton mounts a cogent, radical argument for divorce, an argument informed by the concepts of personal liberty and individual volition, the latter being instrumental in maintaining or ending a marriage. For Milton, marriage depends on the compatibility of the partners, and to maintain a marriage that is without mutual love and sympathy violates one's personal liberty. In such circumstances, the marriage has already ceased. In his later divorce tracts, Milton buttresses his arguments with citations of scholars, such as the 16th-century reformer Martin Bucer, and with biblical passages that he marshals as proof texts.

About the time that the first and second editions of *The Doctrine and Discipline of Divorce* appeared, Milton published *Of Education* (1644). In line with the ideal of the Renaissance gentleman, Milton outlines a curriculum emphasizing the Greek and Latin languages not merely in and of themselves but as the means to learn directly the wisdom of Classical antiquity in literature, philosophy, and politics. The curriculum, which mirrors Milton's own education at St. Paul's, is intended to equip a gentleman to perform "all the offices, both private and public, of peace and war." Aimed at the nobility, not commoners, Milton's plan does not include public education. Nor does it include a university education, possible evidence of Milton's dissatisfaction with Cambridge.

The most renowned tract by Milton is *Areopagitica* (1644), which opposes governmental licensing of publications or procedures of censorship. Milton contends that governments insisting on the expression of uniform beliefs are tyrannical. In his tract, he investigates historical examples of censorship, which, he argues, invariably emanate from repressive governments. The aim of *Areopagitica*, he explains, is to promote knowledge, test experience, and strive for the truth without any hindrances. Milton composed it after the manner of a Classical oration of the same title by Isocrates, directed to the Areopagus, or Athenian council. Informed by Milton's knowledge of Quintilian's *Institutio oratoria* and of orations by Demosthenes and Cicero, *Areopagitica* is a product of the very kind of learning that Milton advocates in *Of Education*. It is ultimately a fierce, passionate defense of the freedom of speech:

For books are not absolutely dead things, but do contain a potency of life in them to be as active as that soul was whose progeny they are. Who kills a man kills a reasonable creature,

God's image; but he who destroys a good book, kills reason
itself, kills the image of God, as it were in the eye.

Counterbalancing the antiprelatical tracts of 1641–42 are the antimonarchical polemics of 1649–55. Composed after Milton had become allied to those who sought to form an English republic, *The Tenure of Kings and Magistrates* (1649)—probably written before and during the trial of King Charles I though not published until after his death on Jan. 30, 1649—urges the abolition of tyrannical kingship and the execution of tyrants. The treatise cites a range of authorities from Classical antiquity, Scripture, the Fathers of the Church, political philosophers of the early modern era, and Reformation theologians, all of whom support such extreme—but just, according to Milton—measures to punish tyrants. Thereafter, Milton was appointed secretary for foreign tongues (also called Latin secretary) for the Council of State, the executive body of the Commonwealth under Oliver Cromwell. Milton was entrusted with the duties of translating foreign correspondence, drafting replies, composing papers in which national and international affairs of state were addressed, and serving as an apologist for the Commonwealth against attacks from abroad.

In this role as an apologist, Milton received the Council of State's assignment to refute *Eikon Basilike* ("Image of the King"), which was published in 1649 within days of the king's beheading. Subtitled *The True Portraiture of His Sacred Majesty in His Solitudes and Sufferings, Eikon Basilike* portrays the late king as pious, contemplative, caring toward his subjects, and gentle toward his family. Though putatively a personal account by Charles himself, the work was written by one of his supporters, Bishop John Gauden, and was very effective in arousing sympathy in England

and on the Continent for the king, whom some perceived as a martyr. In his rebuttal, *Eikonoklastes* (1649; "Image-Breaker"), Milton shatters the image of the king projected in *Eikon Basilike*. Accusing Charles of hypocrisy, Milton cites Shakespeare's portrayal of Richard, duke of Gloucester, in *Richard III* as an analogue that drives home how treachery is disguised by the pretense of piety.

Soon afterward, Milton participated in major controversies against two polemicists on the Continent: Claudius Salmasius (Claude de Saumaise), a Frenchman, and Alexander More (Morus), who was Scottish-French. Charles II, while living in exile in France, is thought to have enlisted Salmasius to compose a Latin tract intended for a Continental audience that would indict the Englishmen who tried and executed Charles I. Universally acknowledged as a reputable scholar, Salmasius posed a formidable challenge to Milton, whose task was to refute his argument. Often imbued with personal invective, Milton's *Defense of the English People Against Salmasius* (1651), a Latin tract, fastens on inconsistencies in Salmasius's argument. Milton echoes much of what he had propounded in earlier tracts: that the execution of a monarch is supported by authorities from Classical antiquity to the early modern era and that public necessity and the tyrannical nature of Charles I's sovereignty justified his death.

In 1652 an anonymous Continental author published another Latin polemic, *The Cry of the King's Blood to Heaven Against the English Parricides*. Milton's refutation in Latin, *The Second Defense of the English People by John Milton, Englishman, in Reply to an Infamous Book Entitled "Cry of the King's Blood"* (1654), contains many autobiographical passages intended to counteract the polemic's vitriolic attacks on his personal life. Milton also mounts an eloquent, idealistic, and impassioned defense of English patriotism and liberty while he extols the leaders of the

Commonwealth. The most poignant passages, however, are reserved for himself. Soon after the publication of *Defense of the English People*, Milton had become totally blind, probably from glaucoma. *The Cry of the King's Blood* asserts that Milton's blindness is God's means of punishing him for his sins. Milton, however, replies that his blindness is a trial that has been visited upon him, an affliction that he is enduring under the approval of the Lord, who has granted him, in turn, special inner illumination, a gift that distinguishes him from others.

MAJOR POEMS

Blind and once a widower, Milton married Katherine Woodcock in 1656. Their marriage lasted only 15 months: she died within months of the birth of their child. He wedded Elizabeth Minshull in 1663, who, along with the daughters from his first marriage, assisted him with his personal needs, read from books at his request, and served as an amanuensis to record verses that he dictated. In the era after the Restoration, Milton published his three major poems, though he had begun work on two of them, *Paradise Lost* and *Samson Agonistes*, many years earlier.

Abandoning his earlier plan to compose an epic on Arthur, Milton instead turned to biblical subject matter and to a Christian idea of heroism. In *Paradise Lost*—first published in 10 books in 1667 and then in 12 books in 1674, at a length of almost 11,000 lines—Milton observed but adapted a number of the Classical epic conventions that distinguish works such as Homer's *The Iliad* and *The Odyssey* and Virgil's *The Aeneid*.

Among these conventions is a focus on the elevated subjects of war, love, and heroism. In Book 6 Milton describes the battle between the good and evil angels. The defeat of the latter results in their expulsion from heaven. In the battle, the Son (Jesus Christ) is invincible in his onslaught against Satan and his cohorts. But Milton's emphasis is less on the Son as a warrior and more on his love for humankind. The Father, in his celestial dialogue with the Son, foresees the sinfulness of Adam and Eve, and the Son chooses to become incarnate and to suffer humbly to redeem them. Though his role as saviour of fallen humankind is not enacted in the epic, Adam and Eve before their expulsion from Eden learn of the future redemptive ministry of Jesus, the exemplary gesture of self-sacrificing love. The Son's selfless love contrasts strikingly with the selfish love of the heroes of Classical epics, who are distinguished by their valour on the battlefield, which is usually incited by pride and vainglory. Their strength and skills on the battlefield and their acquisition of the spoils of war also issue from hate, anger, revenge, greed, and covetousness. If Classical epics deem their protagonists heroic for their extreme passions, even vices, the Son in *Paradise Lost* exemplifies Christian heroism both through his meekness and magnanimity and through his patience and fortitude.

Like many Classical epics, *Paradise Lost* invokes a muse, whom Milton identifies at the outset of the poem:

> *Sing Heav'nly Muse, that on the secret top*
> *Of Horeb, or of Sinai, didst inspire*
> *That shepherd, who first taught the chosen seed,*
> *In the beginning how the heav'ns and earth*
> *Rose out of chaos; or if Sion hill*
> *Delight thee more, and Siloa's brook that flowed*
> *Fast by the oracle of God: I thence*
> *Invoke thy aid to my advent'rous song,*
> *That with no middle flight intends to soar*
> *Above the Aonian mount, while it pursues*
> *Things unattempted yet in prose or rhyme.*

This muse is the Judaeo-Christian Godhead. Citing manifestations of the Godhead atop Horeb and Sinai, Milton seeks inspiration comparable to that visited upon Moses, to whom is ascribed the composition of the book of Genesis. Much as Moses was inspired to recount what he did not witness, so also Milton seeks inspiration to write about biblical events. Recalling Classical epics, in which the haunts of the muses are not only mountaintops but also waterways, Milton cites Siloa's brook, where in the New Testament a blind man acquired sight after going there to wash off the clay and spittle placed over his eyes by Jesus. Likewise, Milton seeks inspiration to enable him to envision and narrate events to which he and all human beings are blind unless chosen for enlightenment by the Godhead. With his reference to "the Aonian mount," or Mt. Helicon in Greece, Milton deliberately invites comparison with Classical antecedents. He avers that his work will supersede these predecessors and will accomplish what has not yet been achieved: a biblical epic in English.

Paradise Lost also directly invokes Classical epics by beginning its action in medias res. Book 1 recounts the aftermath of the war in heaven, which is described only later, in Book 6. At the outset of the epic, the consequences of the loss of the war include the expulsion of the fallen angels from heaven and their descent into hell, a place of infernal torment. With the punishment of the fallen angels having been described early in the epic, Milton in later books recounts how and why their disobedience occurred. Disobedience and its consequences, therefore, come to the fore in Raphael's instruction of Adam and Eve, who (especially in Books 6 and 8) are admonished to remain obedient. By examining the sinfulness of Satan in thought and in deed, Milton positions this part of his narrative close to the temptation of Eve. This arrangement enables Milton to

Satan rouses his fellow fallen angels and other demons to do battle against heavenly forces, in an illustration from the first book of Milton's Paradise Lost. Hulton Archive/Getty Images

highlight how and why Satan, who inhabits a serpent to seduce Eve in Book 9, induces in her the inordinate pride that brought about his own downfall. Satan arouses in Eve a comparable state of mind, which is enacted in her partaking of the forbidden fruit, an act of disobedience.

Milton's epic begins in the hellish underworld and returns there after Satan has tempted Eve to disobedience. In line with Classical depictions of the underworld, Milton emphasizes its darkness, for hell's fires, which are ashen gray, inflict pain but do not provide light. The torments of hell ("on all sides round") also suggest a location like an active volcano. In the Classical tradition, Typhon, who revolted against Jove, was driven down to earth by a thunderbolt, incarcerated under Mt. Aetna in Sicily, and tormented by the fire of this active volcano. Accommodating this Classical analogue to his Christian perception, Milton renders hell chiefly according to biblical accounts, most notably the book of Revelation. The poem's depictions of hell also echo the epic convention of a descent into the underworld.

Throughout *Paradise Lost* Milton uses a grand style aptly suited to the elevated subject matter and tone. In a prefatory note, Milton describes the poem's metre as "English heroic verse without rhyme," which approximates "that of Homer in Greek, and of Virgil in Latin." Rejecting rhyme as "the jingling sound of like endings," Milton prefers a measure that is not end-stopped, so that he may employ enjambment (run-on lines) with "the sense variously drawn out from one verse into another." The grand style that he adopts consists of unrhymed iambic pentameter (blank verse) and features sonorous rhythms pulsating through and beyond one verse into the next. By composing his biblical epic in this measure, he invites comparison with works by Classical forebears. Without using punctuation at the end of many verses, Milton also creates voluble units of rhythm and sense that go well beyond the limitations he perceived in rhymed verse.

Milton also employs other elements of a grand style, most notably epic similes. These explicit comparisons introduced by "like" or "as" proliferate across *Paradise Lost*. Milton tends to add one comparison after another, each one protracted. Accordingly, in one long passage in Book 1, Satan's shield is likened to the Moon as viewed through Galileo's telescope; his spear is larger than the mast of a flagship; the fallen angels outstretched on the lake of fire after their expulsion from heaven "lay entranced / Thick as autumnal leaves that strew the brooks / In Vallombrosa" (literally "Shady Valley," outside Florence). The fallen angels resemble, moreover, the Egyptian cavalry that pursued the Israelites into the parted Red Sea, after which the collapse of the walls of water inundated the Egyptians and left the pharaoh's chariots and charioteers weltering like flotsam.

Paradise Lost is ultimately not only about the downfall of Adam and Eve but also about the clash between Satan and the Son. Many readers have admired Satan's splendid recklessness, if not heroism, in confronting the Godhead. Satan's defiance, anger, willfulness, and resourcefulness define a character who strives never to yield. In many ways Satan is heroic when compared to such Classical prototypes as Achilles, Odysseus, and Aeneas and to similar protagonists in medieval and Renaissance epics. In sum, his traits reflect theirs.

But Milton composed a biblical epic in order to debunk Classical heroism and to extol Christian heroism, exemplified by the Son. Notwithstanding his victory in the battle against the fallen angels, the Son is more heroic because he is willing to undergo voluntary humiliation, a sign of his consummate love for humankind. He foreknows that he will become incarnate in order to suffer death, a selfless act whereby humankind will be redeemed. By such an act, moreover, the Son fulfills what Milton calls the "great argument" of his poem: to "justify the ways of God to man," as Milton writes in Book 1. Despite Satan's success against Adam and Eve, the hope of regeneration after sinfulness is provided by the Son's self-sacrifice. Such hope and opportunity enable humankind to cooperate with the Godhead so as to defeat Satan, avoid damnation, overcome death, and ascend heavenward. Satan's wiles, therefore, are thwarted by members of a regenerate humankind who choose to participate in the redemptive act that the Son has undertaken on their behalf.

Milton's last two poems were published in one volume in 1671. *Paradise Regained*, a brief epic in four books, was followed by *Samson Agonistes*, a dramatic poem not intended for the stage. One story of the composition of *Paradise Regained* derives from Thomas Ellwood, a Quaker who read to the blind Milton and was tutored by him. Ellwood recounts that Milton gave him the manuscript of *Paradise Lost* for examination, and, upon returning it to the poet, who was then residing at Chalfont St. Giles, he commented, "Thou hast said much here of Paradise lost, but what hast thou to say of Paradise found?" Visiting Milton after the poet's return to London from Chalfont St. Giles, Ellwood records that Milton showed him the manuscript of the brief epic and remarked: "This is owing to you; for you put it into my head by the question you put to me at Chalfont, which before I had not thought of." Ellwood's account is not repeated elsewhere, however. It remains unclear whether he embellished his role in the poem's creation.

Paradise Regained hearkens back to the Book of Job, whose principal character is tempted by Satan to forgo his faith in God and to cease exercising patience and fortitude in the midst of ongoing and ever-increasing adversity. By adapting the trials of Job and the role of Satan as tempter and by integrating them with the accounts of Matthew and Luke of Jesus' temptations in the wilderness, Milton dramatizes how Jesus embodies Christian heroism. Less sensational than that of Classical protagonists and not requiring military action for its manifestation, Christian heroism is a continuous reaffirmation of faith in God and is manifested in renewed prayer for patience and fortitude to endure and surmount adversities. By resisting temptations that pander to one's impulses toward ease, pleasure, worldliness, and power, a Christian hero maintains a heavenly orientation that informs his actions. Satan as the tempter in *Paradise Regained* fails in his unceasing endeavours to subvert Jesus by various means in the wilderness. As powerful as the temptations may be, the sophistry that accompanies them is even more insidious.

In effect, *Paradise Regained* unfolds as a series of debates—an ongoing dialectic—in which Jesus analyzes and refutes Satan's arguments. With clarity and cogency, Jesus rebuts any and all arguments by using recta ratio, always informed by faith in God, his father. Strikingly evident also is Jesus' determination, an overwhelming sense of resolve to endure any and all trials visited upon him. Though *Paradise Regained* lacks the vast scope of *Paradise Lost*, it fulfills its purpose admirably by pursuing the idea of Christian heroism as a state of mind. More so than *Paradise Lost*, it dramatizes the inner workings of the mind of Jesus, his perception, and the interplay of faith and reason in his debates with Satan. When Jesus finally dismisses the tempter at the end of the work, the reader recognizes that the encounters in *Paradise Regained* reflect a high degree of psychological verisimilitude.

Like *Paradise Regained*, *Samson Agonistes* focuses on the inner workings of the mind of the protagonist. This emphasis flies in the face of the biblical characterization of Samson in the Book of Judges, which celebrates his physical strength. Milton's dramatic poem, however, begins the story of Samson after his downfall—after he has yielded his God-entrusted secret to Dalila (Delilah), suffered blindness, and become a captive of the Philistines. Tormented by anguish over his captivity, Samson is depressed by the realization that he, the prospective liberator of the Israelites, is now a prisoner, blind and powerless in the hands of his enemies. Samson vacillates from one extreme to another emotionally and psychologically. He becomes depressed, wallows in self-pity, and contemplates suicide. He becomes outraged at himself for having disclosed the secret of his strength. He questions his own nature, whether it was flawed with excessive strength and too little wisdom so that he was destined at birth to suffer eventual downfall. When Dalila visits him during his captivity and offers to minister to him, however, Samson becomes irascible, rejecting her with a harsh diatribe. In doing so, he dramatizes, unwittingly, the measure of his progress toward regeneration. Having succumbed to her previously, he has learned from past experience that Dalila is treacherous.

From that point onward in *Samson Agonistes*, Samson is progressively aroused from depression. He acknowledges that pride in his inordinate strength was a major factor in his downfall and that his previous sense of invincibility rendered him unwary of temptation, even to the extent that he became vulnerable to a woman whose guile charmed him. By the end of the poem, Samson, through expiation and regeneration, has regained a state of spiritual readiness in order to serve again as God's champion. The destruction of the Philistines at the temple of Dagon results in more deaths than the sum of all previous casualties inflicted by Samson. Ironically, when he least expected it, Samson was again chosen to be God's scourge against the Philistines.

Despite Samson's physical feats, Milton depicts him as more heroic during his state of regeneration. Having lapsed into sinfulness when he violated God's command not to disclose the secret of his strength, Samson suffers physically when he is blinded. He also suffers psychologically because he is enslaved by his enemies. The focus of Milton's dramatic poem is ultimately on Samson's regenerative process, an inner struggle beset by torment, by the anxiety that God has rejected him, and by his failure as the would-be liberator of his people.

Unlike the biblical account in Judges, *Samson Agonistes* focuses only on the last day of Samson's life. Discerning that he was victimized by his own pride, Samson becomes chastened and humbled. He becomes acutely aware of the necessity to atone for his sinfulness. In a series of debates not unlike those in *Paradise Regained* between the Son and Satan, Samson engages Manoa, his father; Dalila, his temptress; and Harapha, a stalwart Philistine warrior. In each of these encounters, Samson's discourse manifests an upward trajectory, through atonement and toward regeneration, which culminates in the climactic action at the temple of Dagon where Samson vindicates himself. Echoing *Paradise Lost*, which dramatizes the self-sacrifice of the Son, *Samson Agonistes* creates in its hero an Old Testament prefiguration of the very process of regeneration enabled by the Redeemer and afforded to fallen humankind. In this way, moreover, Samson exhibits the traits of Christian heroism that Milton elsewhere emphasized.

But where the Son of *Paradise Regained* maintains steadfastly his resistance to temptation, Samson typifies human vulnerability to downfall. Accordingly, where in *Paradise Regained* the Son never loses God's favour, *Samson Agonistes* charts how a victim of temptation can reacquire it. Despite the superficial resemblance between his muscular, warlike acts of destruction and those of Classical heroes, Samson is ultimately a Christian hero.

MILTON'S INFLUENCE

After the Restoration and despite jeopardy to himself, Milton continued to advocate freedom of worship and republicanism for England while he supervised the publication of his major poems and other works. For a time soon after the succession of Charles II, Milton was under arrest and menaced by possible execution for involvement in the regicide and in Cromwell's government. Although the circumstances of clemency toward Milton are not fully known, it is likely that certain figures influential with the regime of Charles II—such as Christopher Milton, Andrew Marvell, and William Davenant—interceded on his behalf. The exact date and location of Milton's death remain unknown. He likely died in London on Nov. 8, 1674, from complications of the gout (possibly renal failure). He was buried inside St. Giles Cripplegate Church in London.

Milton's fame and reputation derive chiefly from *Paradise Lost*, which, when first published in 1667, did not gain wide admiration. Because of Milton's political and religious views, only his close friends and associates commended his epic. Marvell, who assisted Milton when he was Latin secretary during the interregnum, expressed extraordinary admiration of *Paradise Lost* in verses at the outset of the 1674 edition. John Dryden, after having consulted with Milton and elicited his approval, adapted the epic to heroic couplets, the measure that characterized much verse in that era. The result was *The State of Innocence and Fall of Man*, an operatic adaptation published in 1677, though never performed. At the end of the 17th century, admiration of *Paradise Lost* extended beyond a small circle. Indeed, five editions of the poem appeared between 1688 and 1698, three of them in English and two in Latin. The 1695 edition in English, with Patrick Hume's commentary and annotations, is considered the first scholarly edition.

By the early 18th century, *Paradise Lost* had begun to draw more acclaim. Joseph Addison published a series of essays in *The Spectator* (1712) in which he ranked Milton's epic with the works of Classical antiquity. Because the Neoclassical movement in poetry, which emphasized heroic couplets, prevailed in this era, *Paradise Lost* was perceived as a magnificent exception in its use of blank verse. And because its genre was that of a biblical epic, *Paradise Lost* was granted unique status. Alexander Pope, the quintessential Neoclassical poet, borrowed heavily from the imagery of Milton's poem and in *The Rape of the Lock* (1712–14) constructed a mock-epic that becomes a genial parody of *Paradise Lost*.

Voltaire lavishly praised *Paradise Lost* in 1727 when writing of epic poetry. Translations of Milton's epic into French, German, and Italian appeared before mid-century. Joseph Warton in 1756 cited Milton's splendid topographical settings, especially Eden in *Paradise Lost*, and praised the flights of sublime imagination that elevated readers into heaven and near the throne of God. In doing so, Warton emphasized two of the poem's characteristics — Milton's celebration of nature and his unbridled imagination — that would later be highly valued by English Romantic authors. But by the end of the 18th century, Milton's reputation had suffered because of Samuel Johnson, whose critical biography in *The Lives of the Poets* (1779–81), while praising the sublimity of *Paradise Lost*, disfavoured Milton's images from nature, which Johnson attributed not to direct experience but to derivations from books.

During the early 19th century, Milton became popular among a number of major Romantic authors, such as William Blake, Percy Bysshe Shelley, and Lord Byron, who in *Paradise Lost* perceived Satan as a heroic rebel opposing established traditions and God as a tyrant. Appropriating elements of Milton's biography and of his works, these authors created a historical and literary context for their own revolutionary ideas. Shelley's Prometheus in *Prometheus Unbound* (1820), for instance, is modeled after Milton's Satan. By the end of the 19th century and into the early 20th century, however, Milton had yet again fallen into disfavour. The most influential voice lessening Milton's reputation was that of T.S. Eliot, whose aesthetic interests gravitated toward the Metaphysical poets, certain Renaissance dramatists, and other contemporaries of Milton. Eliot complained that Milton's epic verse lacked earnest feeling, was "stiff and tortuous," and was so inflexible that it discouraged imitation.

Yet another shift in Milton's reputation occurred in the late 20th century, when the author, while still appreciated for his literary and aesthetic achievements in verse, came to be viewed as a chronicler—even in his poems—of the tensions, conflicts, and upheavals of 17th-century England. At the same time, however, scholars often portrayed Milton variously as a forebear of present-day sensitivities and sensibilities and as an exponent of regressive views. In *Paradise Lost*, for instance, the conjugal relationship between Adam and Eve—both before and after the Fall—is strictly hierarchical, with the husband as overseer of the wife. But this representation of marriage, considered an expression of Milton's regressive views, contrasts with *The Doctrine and Discipline of Divorce*, where Milton contends that the basis of marriage is compatibility. If the partners are no longer compatible, he argues, the marriage is in effect dissolved. Though such a liberal view of divorce was unacceptable in Milton's era, it struck a more responsive chord in those countries where at the turn of the 21st century marriage was understood as a voluntary union between equals. By situating Milton's work within the social, political, and religious currents of his era, scholars, nevertheless, demonstrated the enduring value and modern-day relevance of his works.

CHAPTER 4

ELIZABETHAN AND EARLY STUART DRAMA

I n the Elizabethan and early Stuart period, the theatre was the focal point of the age. Public life was shot through with theatricality—monarchs ruled with ostentatious pageantry, rank and status were defined in a rigid code of dress—while on the stages the tensions and contradictions working to change the nation were embodied and played out. More than any other form, the drama addressed itself to the total experience of its society. Playgoing was inexpensive, and the playhouse yards were thronged with apprentices, fishwives, labourers, and the like, but the same play that was performed to citizen spectators in the afternoon would often be restaged at court by night. The drama's power to activate complex, multiple perspectives on a single issue or event resides in its sensitivity to the competing prejudices and sympathies of this diverse audience.

Moreover, the theatre was fully responsive to the developing technical sophistication of nondramatic literature. In the hands of Shakespeare, the blank verse employed for translation by the earl of Surrey in the first half of the 16th century became a medium infinitely mobile between extremes of formality and intimacy, while prose encompassed both the control of Richard Hooker and the immediacy of Thomas Nashe. This was above all a spoken drama, glorying in the theatrical energies of language. And the stage was able to attract the most technically accomplished writers of its day because it offered, uniquely, a literary career with some realistic prospect of financial return. The decisive event was the opening of the Theatre, considered the first purpose-built London playhouse, in 1576, and during the next 70 years some 20 theatres more are known to have operated. The quantity and diversity of plays they commissioned are little short of astonishing.

THEATRES IN LONDON AND THE PROVINCES

The London theatres were a meeting ground of humanism and popular taste. They inherited, on the one hand, a tradition of humanistic drama current at court, the universities, and the Inns of Court (collegiate institutions responsible for legal education). This tradition involved the revival of Classical plays and attempts to adapt Latin conventions to English, particularly to reproduce the type of tragedy, with its choruses, ghosts, and sententiously formal verse, associated with Seneca (10 tragedies by Seneca in English translation appeared in 1581). A fine example of the type is *Gorboduc* (1561), by Thomas Sackville and Thomas Norton, a tragedy based on British chronicle history that draws for Elizabeth's benefit a grave political moral about irresponsible government. It is also the earliest known English play in blank verse. On the other hand, all the professional companies performing in London continued also to tour in the provinces, and the stage was never allowed to lose contact with its roots in country show, pastime, and festival. The simple moral scheme that pitted virtues against vices in the mid-Tudor interlude was never entirely submerged in more sophisticated drama, and the Vice, the tricksy villain of the morality play, survives, in infinitely more amusing and terrifying form, in Shakespeare's *Richard III* (c. 1592–94).

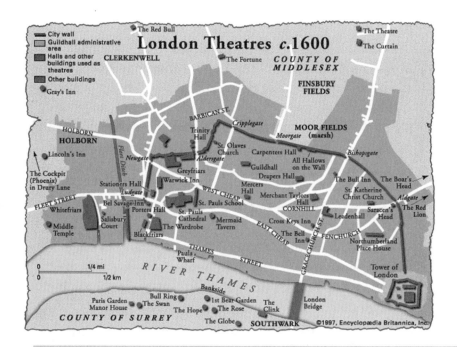

London theatres (c. 1600).

Another survival was the clown or the fool, apt at any moment to step beyond the play's illusion and share jokes directly with the spectators. The intermingling of traditions is clear in two farces, Nicholas Udall's *Ralph Roister Doister* (1553) and the anonymous *Gammer Gurton's Needle* (1559), in which academic pastiche is overlaid with country game. And what the popular tradition did for tragedy is indicated in Thomas Preston's *Cambises, King of Persia* (c. 1560), a blood-and-thunder tyrant play with plenty of energetic spectacle and comedy.

A third tradition was that of revelry and masques, practiced at the princely courts across Europe and preserved in England in the witty and impudent productions of the schoolboy troupes of choristers who sometimes played in London alongside the professionals. An early play related to this kind is the first English prose comedy, Gascoigne's *Supposes* (1566), translated from a reveling play in Italian. Courtly revel reached its apogee in England in the ruinously expensive court masques staged for James I and Charles I, magnificent displays of song, dance, and changing scenery performed before a tiny aristocratic audience and glorifying the king. The principal masque writer was Ben Jonson, the scene designer Inigo Jones.

PROFESSIONAL PLAYWRIGHTS

The first generation of professional playwrights in England has become known collectively as the university wits. Their nickname identifies their social pretensions, but their drama was primarily middle class, patriotic, and romantic. Their preferred subjects were historical or pseudo-historical, mixed with clowning, music, and love interest. At times, plot virtually evaporated. George Peele's *Old Wives' Tale* (c. 1595) and Nashe's *Summer's Last Will and Testament* (1600) are simply popular shows, charming medleys of comic turns, spectacle, and song. Peele was a civic poet, and his serious plays are bold and pageantlike. *The Arraignment of Paris* (1584) is a pastoral entertainment, designed to compliment Elizabeth. Robert Greene's speciality was comical histories, interweaving a serious plot set among kings with comic action involving clowns. In his *Friar Bacon and Friar Bungay* (1594) and *James IV* (1598), the antics of vulgar characters complement but also criticize the follies of their betters. Only John Lyly, writing for the choristers, endeavoured to achieve a courtly refinement. His *Gallathea* (1584) and *Endimion* (1591) are fantastic comedies in which courtiers, nymphs, and goddesses make rarefied love in intricate, artificial patterns, the very stuff of courtly dreaming.

Blank Verse

Blank verse is unrhymed iambic pentameter, the preeminent dramatic and narrative verse form in English. A line of blank verse, in English, consists of five metrical feet (hence the name pentameter) in which one unstressed syllable is followed by one long or stressed syllable, these two syllables together forming a metrical foot known as an iamb. The richness and versatility of blank verse depends on the skill of the poet in varying the stresses and the position of the caesura (pause) in each line, in catching the shifting tonal qualities and emotional overtones of the language, and in arranging lines into thought groups and paragraphs.

Adapted from unrhymed Greek and Latin heroic verse, blank verse was introduced in 16th-century Italy along with other classical metres. The Italian humanist Francesco Maria Molza attempted the writing of consecutive unrhymed verse in 1514 in his translation of Virgil's *Aeneid*. Other experiments in 16th-century Italy were the tragedy *Sofonisba* (written 1514–15) by Gian Giorgio Trissino, and the didactic poem *Le api* (1539) by Giovanni Rucellai. Rucellai was the first to use the term *versi sciolti*, which became translated into English as "blank verse." It soon became the standard metre of Italian Renaissance drama, used in such major works as the comedies of Ludovico Ariosto, *L'Aminta* of Torquato Tasso, and the *Il pastor fido* of Battista Guarini.

Henry Howard, earl of Surrey, introduced the metre, along with the sonnet and other Italian humanist verse forms, to England in the early 16th century. Thomas Sackville and Thomas Norton used blank verse for the first English tragic drama, *Gorboduc* (first performed 1561), and Christopher Marlowe developed its musical qualities and emotional power in *Tamburlaine, Doctor Faustus*, and *Edward II*. William Shakespeare transformed the line and the instrument of blank verse into the vehicle for the greatest English dramatic poetry. In his early plays, he combined it with prose and a 10-syllable rhymed couplet; he later employed a blank verse dependent on stress rather than on syllabic length. Shakespeare's poetic expression in his later plays, such as *Hamlet, King Lear, Othello, Macbeth,* and *The Winter's Tale*, is supple, approximating the rhythms of speech, yet capable of conveying the subtlest human delight, grief, or perplexity.

CHRISTOPHER MARLOWE

Outshining all the university wits is Christopher Marlowe, who alone realized the tragic potential inherent in the popular style, with its bombast and extravagance.

Marlowe was the second child and eldest son of John Marlowe, a Canterbury shoemaker. Nothing is known of his first schooling, but on Jan. 14, 1579, he entered the King's School, Canterbury, as a scholar. A year later he went to Corpus Christi College, Cambridge. Obtaining his bachelor of arts degree in 1584, he continued in residence at Cambridge, which may imply that he was intending to take Anglican orders. In 1587, however, the university hesitated about granting him a master's degree. Its doubts (arising from his frequent absences from the university) were apparently set at rest when the Privy Council sent a letter declaring that he had been employed "on matters touching the benefit of his country"—apparently in Elizabeth I's secret service.

After 1587, Marlowe was in London, writing for the theatres, occasionally getting into trouble with the authorities because of his violent and disreputable behaviour, and probably also engaging himself from time to time in government service. Marlowe won a dangerous reputation for "atheism," but this could, in Elizabeth I's time, indicate merely unorthodox religious opinions. In Robert Greene's deathbed tract, *Greenes groats-worth of witte,*

In a scant six-year time frame, the tempestuous playwright Christopher Marlowe substantially altered the course of English drama. Marlowe is most noted for the establishment of dramatic blank verse. Keystone/Hulton Archive/ Getty Images

Marlowe is referred to as a "famous gracer of Tragedians" and is reproved for having said, like Greene himself, "There is no god" and for having studied "pestilent Machiuilian pollicie." There is further evidence of his unorthodoxy, notably in the denunciation of him written by the spy Richard Baines and in the letter of Thomas Kyd to the lord keeper in 1593 after Marlowe's death. Kyd alleged that certain papers "denying the deity of Jesus Christ" that were found in his room belonged to Marlowe, who had shared the room two years before. Both Baines and Kyd suggested on Marlowe's part atheism in the stricter sense and a persistent delight in blasphemy.

Whatever the case may be, on May 18, 1593, the Privy Council issued an order for Marlowe's arrest. Two days later the poet was ordered to give daily attendance on their lordships "until he shall be licensed to the contrary." On May 30, however, Marlowe was killed by Ingram Frizer, in the dubious company of Nicholas Skeres and Robert Poley, at a lodging house in Deptford, where they had spent most of the day and where, it was alleged, a fight broke out between them over the bill.

MARLOWE'S WORKS

In the earliest of Marlowe's plays, the two-part *Tamburlaine the Great* (c. 1587; published 1590), Marlowe's characteristic "mighty line" (as Ben Jonson called it) established blank verse as the staple medium for later Elizabethan and Jacobean dramatic writing. It appears that originally Marlowe intended to write only the first part, concluding with Tamburlaine's marriage to Zenocrate and his making "truce with all the world." But the popularity of the first part encouraged Marlowe to continue the story to Tamburlaine's death. This gave him some difficulty, as he had almost exhausted his historical sources in part I;

Faust, detail from the title page of the 1616 edition of The Tragicall History of Dr. Faustus *by Christopher Marlowe.* Courtesy of the trustees of the British Library; photograph, R.B. Fleming

consequently the sequel has, at first glance, an appearance of padding. Yet the effort demanded in writing the continuation made the young playwright look more coldly and searchingly at the hero he had chosen, and thus part II makes explicit certain notions that were below the surface and insufficiently recognized by the dramatist in part I.

Marlowe's most famous play, *The Tragicall History of Dr. Faustus,* has survived only in a corrupt form, and its date of composition has been much-disputed. It was first published in 1604, and another version appeared in 1616. *Faustus* takes over the dramatic framework of the morality plays in its presentation of a story of temptation, fall, and damnation and its free use of morality figures such as the good angel and the bad angel and the seven deadly sins, along with the devils Lucifer and Mephistopheles. In *Faustus* Marlowe tells the story of the doctor-turned-necromancer Faustus, who sells his soul to the devil in exchange for knowledge and power. The devil's intermediary in the play, Mephistopheles, achieves tragic grandeur in his own right as a fallen angel torn between satanic pride and dark despair.

Just as in *Tamburlaine* Marlowe had seen the cruelty and absurdity of his hero as well as his magnificence, so here he can enter into Faustus's grandiose intellectual ambition, simultaneously viewing those ambitions as futile, self-destructive, and absurd. The text is problematic in the low comic scenes spuriously introduced by later hack writers, but its more sober and consistent moments are certainly the uncorrupted work of Marlowe.

In *The Famous Tragedy of the Rich Jew of Malta*, Marlowe portrays another power-hungry figure in the Jew Barabas, who in the villainous society of Christian Malta shows no scruple in self-advancement. But this figure is more closely incorporated within his society than either Tamburlaine, the supreme conqueror, or Faustus, the lonely adventurer against God. In the end Barabas is overcome, not by a divine stroke but by the concerted action of his human enemies. There is a difficulty in deciding how fully the extant text of *The Jew of Malta* represents Marlowe's original play, for it was not published until 1633. But *The Jew* can be closely associated with *The Massacre at Paris* (1593), a dramatic presentation of incidents from contemporary French history, including the Massacre of St. Bartholomew's Day, and with *The Troublesome Raigne and Lamentable Death of Edward the Second* (published 1594), Marlowe's great contribution to the Elizabethan plays on historical themes.

As *The Massacre* introduces in the duke of Guise a figure unscrupulously avid for power, so in the younger Mortimer or *Edward II*, Marlowe shows a man developing an appetite for power and increasingly corrupted as power comes to him. In each instance the dramatist shares in the excitement of the pursuit of glory, but all three plays present such figures within a social framework: the notion of social responsibility, the notion of corruption through power, and the notion of the suffering that the exercise of power entails are all prominently the dramatist's concern. Apart from *Tamburlaine* and the minor work *Dido, Queen of Carthage* (of uncertain date, published 1594 and written in collaboration with Thomas Nashe, *Edward II* is the only one of Marlowe's plays whose extant text can be relied on as adequately representing the author's manuscript. And certainly *Edward II* is a major work, not merely one of the first Elizabethan plays on an English historical theme. The relationships linking the king, his neglected queen, the king's favourite, Gaveston, and the ambitious Mortimer are studied with detached sympathy and remarkable understanding: no character here is lightly disposed of, and the abdication and the brutal murder of Edward show the same dark and violent imagination as appeared in Marlowe's presentation of Faustus' last hour. Though this play, along with *The Jew* and *The Massacre,* shows Marlowe's fascinated response to the distorted Elizabethan idea of Machiavelli, it more importantly shows Marlowe's deeply suggestive awareness of the nature of disaster, the power of society, and the dark extent of an individual's suffering.

In addition to translations (Ovid's *Amores* and the first book of Lucan's *Pharsalia*), Marlowe's nondramatic work includes the poem *Hero and Leander*. This work was incomplete at his death and was extended by George Chapman; the joint work of the two poets was published in 1598.

LITERARY CAREER

In a playwriting career that spanned little more than six years, Marlowe's achievements were diverse and splendid. Perhaps before leaving Cambridge he had already written *Tamburlaine the Great* (in two parts, both performed by the end of 1587; published 1590). Almost certainly during his later Cambridge years, Marlowe had translated Ovid's *Amores* (*The Loves*) and the first book of Lucan's *Pharsalia* from the Latin. About this time he also wrote the play *Dido, Queen of Carthage* (published in 1594 as the joint work of Marlowe and Thomas Nashe). With the production of *Tamburlaine* he received recognition and acclaim, and playwriting became his major concern in the few years that lay ahead. Both parts of *Tamburlaine* were published anonymously in 1590, and the publisher omitted certain passages that he found incongruous with the play's serious concern with history. Even so, the extant *Tamburlaine* text can be regarded as substantially Marlowe's. No other of his plays or poems or translations was published during his life. His unfinished but splendid poem *Hero and Leander*—which is almost certainly the finest nondramatic Elizabethan poem apart from those produced by Edmund Spenser—appeared in 1598.

There is argument among scholars concerning the order in which the plays subsequent to *Tamburlaine* were written. It is not uncommonly held that *Faustus* quickly followed *Tamburlaine* and that then Marlowe turned to a more neutral, more "social" kind of writing in *Edward II* and *The Massacre at Paris*. His last play may have been *The Jew of Malta*, in which he signally broke new ground. It is known that *Tamburlaine, Faustus,* and *The Jew of Malta* were performed by the Admiral's Men, a company whose outstanding actor was Edward Alleyn, who most certainly played Tamburlaine, Faustus, and Barabas the Jew.

ASSESSMENT

Marlowe's heroes are men of towering ambition who speak blank verse of unprecedented (and occasionally monotonous) elevation, their "high astounding terms" embodying the challenge that they pose to the orthodox values of the societies they disrupt. In *Tamburlaine the Great* and *Edward II*, traditional political orders are overwhelmed by conquerors and politicians who ignore the boasted legitimacy of weak kings. *The Jew of Malta* studies the man of business whose financial acumen and trickery give him unrestrained power. Faustus depicts the overthrow of a man whose learning shows scant regard for God.

The main focus of all these plays is on the uselessness of society's moral and religious sanctions against pragmatic, amoral will. They patently address themselves to the anxieties of an age being transformed by new forces in politics, commerce, and science. Indeed, the sinister, ironic prologue to *The Jew of Malta* is spoken by Machiavelli. In his own time Marlowe was damned as atheist, homosexual, and libertine, and his plays remain disturbing because his verse makes theatrical presence into the expression of power, enlisting the spectators' sympathies on the side of his gigantic villain-heroes. His plays thus present the spectator with dilemmas that can be neither resolved nor ignored, and they articulate exactly the divided consciousness of their time. There is a similar effect in Kyd's *The Spanish Tragedy*, an early revenge tragedy in which the hero seeks justice for the loss of his son but, in an unjust world, can achieve it only by taking the law into his own hands. Kyd's use of Senecan conventions (notably a ghost impatient for revenge) in a Christian setting expresses a genuine conflict of values, making the hero's success at once triumphant and horrifying.

Painting first identified as depicting William Shakespeare in 2009. Shakespeare was an equally nimble poet and actor as well as one of the greatest dramatists of all time. His work defies cultural boundaries and is read and performed worldwide to this day. Oli Scarff/Getty Images

WILLIAM SHAKESPEARE

Above all other dramatists stands William Shakespeare, a supreme genius whom it is impossible to characterize briefly. Shakespeare is unequaled as poet and intellect, but he remains elusive. His capacity for assimilation—what the poet John Keats called his "negative capability"—means that his work is comprehensively accommodating. Every attitude or ideology finds its resemblance there yet also finds itself subject to criticism and interrogation. In part, Shakespeare achieved this by the total inclusiveness of his aesthetic, by putting clowns in his tragedies and kings in his comedies, juxtaposing public and private, and mingling the artful with the spontaneous. His plays imitate the counterchange of values occurring at large in his society. The sureness and profound popularity of his taste enabled him to lead the English Renaissance without privileging or prejudicing any one of its divergent aspects, while he—as actor, dramatist, and shareholder in the Lord Chamberlain's players—was involved in the Elizabethan theatre at every level. His career (dated from 1589 to 1613) corresponded exactly to the period of greatest literary flourishing, and only in his work are the total possibilities of the Renaissance fully realized.

SHAKESPEARE THE MAN

Although the amount of factual knowledge available about Shakespeare is surprisingly large for one of his station in life, many find it disappointing, for it is mostly gleaned from documents of an official character. There are, however, many contemporary allusions to him as a writer, and these add a reasonable amount of flesh and blood to the biographical skeleton.

Anne Hathaway's house, near Stratford-upon-Avon, Warwickshire. She married Shakespeare in 1582, when she was 26 and he was 18, and remained in Stratford while he lived and worked in London. SSPL/Getty Images

EARLY LIFE IN STRATFORD

The parish register of Holy Trinity Church in Stratford-upon-Avon, Warwickshire, shows that he was baptized there on April 26, 1564. His birthday is traditionally celebrated on April 23. His father, John Shakespeare, was a burgess of the borough, who in 1565 was chosen an alderman and in 1568 bailiff (the position corresponding to mayor, before the grant of a further charter to Stratford in 1664). He was engaged in various kinds of trade and appears to have suffered some fluctuations in prosperity. His wife, Mary Arden, of Wilmcote, Warwickshire, came from an ancient family and was the heiress to some land. (Given the somewhat rigid social distinctions of the 16th century, this marriage must have been a step up the social scale for John Shakespeare.)

Stratford enjoyed a grammar school of good quality, and the education there was free, the schoolmaster's salary being paid by the borough. No lists of the pupils who were at the school in the 16th century have survived, but it would be absurd to suppose the bailiff of the town did not send his son there. The boy's education would consist mostly of Latin studies—learning to read, write, and speak the language fairly well and studying some of the Classical historians, moralists, and poets. Shakespeare did not go on to the university, and indeed it is unlikely that the scholarly round of logic, rhetoric, and other studies then followed there would have interested him.

Instead, at age 18 he married. Where and exactly when are not known, but the episcopal registry at Worcester preserves a bond dated Nov. 28, 1582, and executed by two yeomen of Stratford, named Sandells and Richardson, as a security to the bishop for the issue of a license for the marriage of William Shakespeare and "Anne Hathaway of Stratford," upon the consent of her friends and upon once asking of the banns. (Anne died in 1623, seven years after Shakespeare. There is good evidence to associate her with a family of Hathaways who inhabited a beautiful farmhouse, now much visited, 2 miles [3.2 km] from Stratford.) The next date of interest is found in the records of the Stratford church, where a daughter, named Susanna, born to William Shakespeare, was baptized on May 26, 1583. On Feb. 2, 1585, twins were baptized, Hamnet and Judith. (Hamnet, Shakespeare's only son, died 11 years later.)

How Shakespeare spent the next eight years or so, until his name begins to appear in London theatre records, is not known. There are stories—given currency long after his death—of stealing deer and getting into trouble with a local magnate, Sir Thomas Lucy of Charlecote, near Stratford; of earning his living as a schoolmaster in the country; of going to London and gaining entry to the world of theatre by minding the horses of theatregoers. It has also been conjectured that Shakespeare spent some time as a member of a great household and that he was a soldier, perhaps in the Low Countries. In lieu of external evidence, such extrapolations about Shakespeare's life have often been made from the internal "evidence" of his writings. But this method is unsatisfactory: one cannot conclude, for example, from his allusions to the law that Shakespeare was a lawyer, for he was clearly a writer who without difficulty could get whatever knowledge he needed for the composition of his plays.

CAREER IN THE THEATRE

The first reference to Shakespeare in the literary world of London comes in 1592, when a fellow dramatist, Robert Greene, declared in a pamphlet written on his deathbed: "There is an upstart crow, beautified with our feathers, that with his *Tygers heart wrapt in a Players hide* supposes he is as well able to bombast out a blank verse as the best of you; and, being an absolute *Johannes Factotum*, is in his own conceit the only Shake-scene in a country."

What these words mean is difficult to determine, but clearly they are insulting, and clearly Shakespeare is the object of the sarcasms. When the book in which they appear (*Greenes, groats-worth of witte, bought with a million of Repentance*, 1592) was published after Greene's death, a mutual acquaintance wrote a preface offering an apology to Shakespeare and testifying to his worth. This preface also indicates that Shakespeare was by then making important friends. For, although the puritanical city of London was generally hostile to the theatre, many of the nobility were good patrons of the drama and friends of the actors. Shakespeare seems to have attracted the attention of the young Henry Wriothesley, the 3rd earl of

Southampton, and to this nobleman were dedicated his first published poems, *Venus and Adonis* and *The Rape of Lucrece*.

One striking piece of evidence that Shakespeare began to prosper early and tried to retrieve the family's fortunes and establish its gentility is the fact that a coat of arms was granted to John Shakespeare in 1596. Rough drafts of this grant have been preserved in the College of Arms, London, though the final document, which must have been handed to the Shakespeares, has not survived. Almost certainly William himself took the initiative and paid the fees. The coat of arms appears on Shakespeare's monument (constructed before 1623) in the Stratford church. Equally interesting as evidence of Shakespeare's worldly success was his purchase in 1597 of New Place, a large house in Stratford, which he as a boy must have passed every day in walking to school.

How his career in the theatre began is unclear, but from roughly 1594 onward he was an important member of the Lord Chamberlain's company of players (called the King's Men after the accession of James I in 1603). They had the best actor, Richard Burbage. They had the best theatre, the Globe (finished by the autumn of 1599), and they had the best dramatist, Shakespeare. It is no wonder that the company prospered. Shakespeare became a full-time professional man of his own theatre, sharing in a cooperative enterprise and intimately concerned with the financial success of the plays he wrote.

Unfortunately, written records give little indication of the way in which Shakespeare's professional life molded his marvelous artistry. All that can be deduced is that for 20 years Shakespeare devoted himself assiduously to his art, writing more than a million words of poetic drama of the highest quality.

PRIVATE LIFE

Shakespeare had little contact with officialdom, apart from walking—dressed in the royal livery as a member of the King's Men—at the coronation of King James I in 1604. He continued to look after his financial interests. He bought properties in London and in Stratford. In 1605 he purchased a share (about one-fifth) of the Stratford tithes—a fact that explains why he was eventually buried in the chancel of its parish church. For some time he lodged with a French Huguenot family called Mountjoy, who lived near St. Olave's Church in Cripplegate, London. The records of a lawsuit in May 1612, resulting from a Mountjoy family quarrel, show Shakespeare as giving evidence in a genial way (though unable to remember certain important facts that would have decided the case) and as interesting himself generally in the family's affairs.

No letters written by Shakespeare have survived, but a private letter to him happened to get caught up with some official transactions of the town of Stratford and so has been preserved in the borough archives. It was written by one Richard Quiney and addressed by him from the Bell Inn in Carter Lane, London, whither he had gone from Stratford on business. On one side of the paper is inscribed: "To my loving good friend and countryman, Mr. Wm. Shakespeare, deliver these." Apparently Quiney thought his fellow Stratfordian a person to whom he could apply for the loan of £30—a large sum in Elizabethan times. Nothing further is known about the transaction, but, because so few opportunities of seeing into Shakespeare's private life present themselves, this begging letter becomes a touching document. It is of some interest, moreover, that 18 years later Quiney's son Thomas became the husband of Judith, Shakespeare's second daughter.

Shakespeare's will (made on March 25, 1616) is a long and detailed document. It entailed his quite ample property on the male heirs of his elder daughter, Susanna. (Both his daughters were then married, one to the aforementioned Thomas Quiney and the other to John Hall, a respected physician of Stratford.) As an afterthought, he bequeathed his "second-best bed" to his wife. No one can be certain what this notorious legacy means. The testator's signatures to the will are apparently in a shaky hand. Perhaps Shakespeare was already ill. He died on April 23, 1616. No name was inscribed on his gravestone in the chancel of the parish church of Stratford-upon-Avon. Instead these lines, possibly his own, appeared:

Good friend, for Jesus' sake forbear
To dig the dust enclosed here.
Blest be the man that spares these stones,
And curst be he that moves my bones.

SHAKESPEARE'S EARLY PLAYS

Shakespeare arrived in London probably sometime in the late 1580s. He was in his mid-20s. It is not known how he got started in the theatre or for what acting companies he wrote his early plays, which are not easy to date. Indicating a time of apprenticeship, these plays show a more direct debt to London dramatists of the 1580s and to Classical examples than do his later works. He learned a great deal about writing plays by imitating the successes of the London theatre, as any young poet and budding dramatist might do.

TITUS ANDRONICUS

Titus Andronicus (c. 1589–92) is a case in point. As Shakespeare's first full-length tragedy, it owes much of its theme, structure, and language to Thomas Kyd's *The Spanish Tragedy*, which was a huge success in the late 1580s. Kyd had hit on the formula of adopting the dramaturgy of Seneca (the younger), the great Stoic philosopher and statesman, to the needs of a burgeoning new London theatre. The result was the revenge tragedy, an astonishingly successful genre that was to be refigured in *Hamlet* and many other revenge plays. Shakespeare also borrowed a leaf from his great contemporary Christopher Marlowe. The Vice-like protagonist of Marlowe's *The Jew of Malta*, Barabas, may have inspired Shakespeare in his depiction of the villainous Aaron the Moor in *Titus Andronicus*, though other Vice figures were available to him as well.

The Senecan model offered Kyd, and then Shakespeare, a story of bloody revenge, occasioned originally by the murder or rape of a person whose near relatives (fathers, sons, brothers) are bound by sacred oath to revenge the atrocity. The avenger must proceed with caution, since his opponent is canny, secretive, and ruthless. The avenger becomes mad or feigns madness to cover his intent. He becomes more and more ruthless himself as he moves toward his goal of vengeance. At the same time he is hesitant, being deeply distressed by ethical considerations. An ethos of revenge is opposed to one of Christian forbearance. The avenger may see the spirit of the person whose wrongful death he must avenge. He employs the device of a play within the play in order to accomplish his aims. The play ends in a bloodbath and a vindication of the avenger. Evident in this model is the story of *Titus Andronicus*, whose sons are butchered and whose daughter is raped and mutilated, as well as the story of Hamlet and still others.

THE EARLY ROMANTIC COMEDIES

Other than *Titus Andronicus*, Shakespeare did not experiment with formal tragedy in his early years. (Though his

English history plays from this period portrayed tragic events, their theme was focused elsewhere.) The young playwright was drawn more quickly into comedy, and with more immediate success. For this his models include the dramatists Robert Greene and John Lyly, along with Thomas Nashe. The result is a genre recognizably and distinctively Shakespearean, even if he learned a lot from Greene and Lyly: the romantic comedy.

As in the work of his models, Shakespeare's early comedies revel in stories of amorous courtship in which a plucky and admirable young woman (played by a boy actor) is paired off against her male wooer. Julia, one of two young heroines in *The Two Gentlemen of Verona* (*c.* 1590–94), disguises herself as a man in order to follow her lover, Proteus, when he is sent from Verona to Milan. Proteus (appropriately named for the changeable Proteus of Greek myth), she discovers, is paying far too much attention to Sylvia, the beloved of Proteus's best friend, Valentine. Love and friendship thus do battle for the divided loyalties of the erring male until the generosity of his friend and, most of all, the enduring chaste loyalty of the two women bring Proteus to his senses. The motif of the young woman disguised as a male was to prove invaluable to Shakespeare in subsequent romantic comedies, including *The Merchant of Venice, As You Like It,* and *Twelfth Night.* As is generally true of Shakespeare, he derived the essentials of his plot from a narrative source, in this case a long Spanish prose romance, the *Diana* of Jorge de Montemayor.

Shakespeare's most classically inspired early comedy is *The Comedy of Errors* (*c.* 1589–94). Here he turned particularly to Plautus's farcical play called the *Menaechmi* ("Twins"). The story of one twin (Antipholus) looking for his lost brother, accompanied by a clever servant (Dromio) whose twin has also disappeared, results in a farce of mistaken identities that also thoughtfully explores issues of identity and self-knowing. The young women of the play, one the wife of Antipholus of Ephesus (Adriana) and the other her sister (Luciana), engage in meaningful dialogue on issues of wifely obedience and autonomy. Marriage resolves these difficulties at the end, as is routinely the case in Shakespearean romantic comedy, but not before the plot complications have tested the characters' needs to know who they are and what men and women ought to expect from one another.

Shakespeare's early romantic comedy most indebted to John Lyly is *Love's Labour's Lost* (c. 1588–97), a confection set in the never-never land of Navarre where the King and his companions are visited by the Princess of France and her ladies-in-waiting on a diplomatic mission that soon devolves into a game of courtship. As is often the case in Shakespearean romantic comedy, the young women are sure of who they are and whom they intend to marry. One cannot be certain that they ever really fall in love, since they begin by knowing what they want. The young men, conversely, fall all over themselves in their comically futile attempts to eschew romantic love in favour of more serious pursuits. They perjure themselves, are shamed and put down, and are finally forgiven their follies by the women. Shakespeare brilliantly portrays male discomfiture and female self-assurance as he explores the treacherous but desirable world of sexual attraction, while the verbal gymnastics of the play emphasize the wonder and the delicious foolishness of falling in love.

In *The Taming of the Shrew* (c. 1590–94), Shakespeare employs a device of multiple plotting that is to become a standard feature of his romantic comedies. In one plot, derived from Ludovico Ariosto's *I suppositi* (*Supposes*, as it had been translated into English by George Gascoigne), a young woman (Bianca) carries on a risky courtship with a young man who appears to be a tutor, much to the dismay of her father, who hopes to marry her to a wealthy suitor of his own choosing. Eventually the mistaken identities are straightened out, establishing the presumed tutor as Lucentio, wealthy and suitable enough. Simultaneously, Bianca's shrewish sister Kate denounces (and terrorizes) all men. Bianca's suitors commission the self-assured Petruchio to pursue Kate so that Bianca, the younger sister, will be free to wed. The wife-taming plot is itself based on folktale and ballad tradition in which men assure their ascendancy in the marriage relationship by beating their wives into submission. Shakespeare transforms this raw, antifeminist material into a study of the struggle for dominance in the marriage relationship. And, whereas he does opt in this play for male triumph over the female, he gives to Kate a sense of humour that enables her to see how she is to play the game to her own advantage as well. She is, arguably, happy at the end with a relationship based on wit and companionship, whereas her sister Bianca turns out to be simply spoiled.

The Early Histories

In Shakespeare's explorations of English history, as in romantic comedy, he put his distinctive mark on a genre and made it his. The genre was, moreover, an unusual one. There was as yet no definition of an English history play, and there were no aesthetic rules regarding its shaping. The ancient Classical world had recognized two broad categories of genre, comedy and tragedy. (This account leaves out more specialized genres like the satyr play.) Aristotle and other critics, including Horace, had evolved, over centuries, Classical definitions. Tragedy dealt with the disaster-struck lives of great persons, was written in elevated verse, and took as its setting a mythological and ancient world of gods and heroes: Agamemnon, Theseus, Oedipus, Medea, and the rest. Pity and terror were the prevailing emotional responses in plays that sought to understand, however imperfectly, the will of the supreme gods. Classical comedy, conversely, dramatized the everyday. Its chief figures were citizens of Athens and Rome—householders, courtesans, slaves, scoundrels, and so forth. The humour was immediate, contemporary, topical. The lampooning was satirical, even savage. Members of the audience were invited to look at mimetic representations of their own daily lives and to laugh at greed and folly.

The English history play had no such ideal theoretical structure. It was an existential invention: the dramatic treatment of recent English history. It might be tragic or comic or, more commonly, a hybrid. Polonius's list of generic possibilities captures the ludicrous potential for endless hybridizations: "tragedy, comedy, history, pastoral, pastoral-comical, historical-pastoral, tragical-historical, tragical-comical-historical-pastoral," and so on (*Hamlet*, Act II, scene 2, lines 397–399). (By "pastoral," Polonius presumably means a play based on romances telling of shepherds and rural life, as contrasted with the corruptions of city and court.) Shakespeare's history plays were so successful in the 1590s' London theatre that the editors of Shakespeare's complete works, in 1623, chose to group his dramatic output under three headings: comedies, histories, and tragedies. The genre established itself by sheer force of its compelling popularity.

Shakespeare in 1590 or thereabouts had really only one viable model for the English history play, an anonymous and sprawling drama called *The Famous Victories of Henry the Fifth* (1583–88) that told the saga of Henry IV's son, Prince Hal, from the days of his adolescent rebellion down through his victory over the French at the Battle of Agincourt in 1415—in other words, the material that Shakespeare would later use in writing three major plays,

Henry IV, Part 1; *Henry IV, Part 2*; and *Henry V*. Shakespeare chose to start not with Prince Hal but with more recent history in the reign of Henry V's son Henry VI and with the civil wars that saw the overthrow of Henry VI by Edward IV and then the accession to power in 1483 of Richard III. This material proved to be so rich in themes and dramatic conflicts that he wrote four plays on it, a "tetralogy" extending from *Henry VI* in three parts (*c.* 1589–93) to *Richard III* (*c.* 1592–94).

These plays were immediately successful. Contemporary references indicate that audiences of the early 1590s thrilled to the story (in *Henry VI, Part 1*) of the brave Lord Talbot doing battle in France against the witch Joan of Arc and her lover, the French Dauphin, but being undermined in his heroic effort by effeminacy and corruption at home. Henry VI himself is, as Shakespeare portrays him, a weak king, raised to the kingship by the early death of his father, incapable of controlling factionalism in his court, and enervated personally by his infatuation with a dangerous Frenchwoman, Margaret of Anjou. Henry VI is cuckolded by his wife and her lover, the Duke of Suffolk, and (in *Henry VI, Part 2*) proves unable to defend his virtuous uncle, the Duke of Gloucester, against opportunistic enemies. The result is civil unrest, lower-class rebellion (led by Jack Cade), and eventually all-out civil war between the Lancastrian faction, nominally headed by Henry VI, and the Yorkist claimants under the leadership of Edward IV and his brothers. *Richard III* completes the saga with its account of the baleful rise of Richard of Gloucester through the murdering of his brother the Duke of Clarence and of Edward IV's two sons, who were also Richard's nephews. Richard's tyrannical reign yields eventually and inevitably to the newest and most successful claimant of the throne, Henry Tudor, earl of Richmond. This is the man who becomes Henry VII, scion of the Tudor dynasty

An 18th-century engraving depicting a scene from Shakespeare's play Richard III, *where the villainous Richard has his nephews murdered so that he may wear the crown.* Richard III *was the final play in his "first tetralogy" on English history, which describes events during the late 14th and early 15th centuries.* Kean Collection/Hulton Archive/Getty Images

and grandfather of Queen Elizabeth I, who reigned from 1558 to 1603 and hence during the entire first decade and more of Shakespeare's productive career.

The Shakespearean English history play told of the country's history at a time when the English nation was struggling with its own sense of national identity and experiencing a new sense of power. Queen Elizabeth had brought stability and a relative freedom from war to her decades of rule. She had held at bay the Roman Catholic powers of the Continent, notably Philip II of Spain, and, with the help of a storm at sea, had fought off Philip's attempts to invade her kingdom with the great Spanish Armada of 1588. In England the triumph of the nation was viewed universally as a divine deliverance. The second edition of Holinshed's *Chronicles* was at hand as a vast source for Shakespeare's historical playwriting. It, too, celebrated the emergence of England as a major Protestant power, led by a popular and astute monarch.

From the perspective of the 1590s, the history of the 15th century also seemed newly pertinent. England had emerged from a terrible civil war in 1485, with Henry Tudor's victory over Richard III at the Battle of Bosworth Field. The chief personages of these wars, known as the Wars of the Roses — Henry Tudor, Richard III, the duke of Buckingham, Hastings, Rivers, Gray, and many more — were very familiar to contemporary English readers.

Because these historical plays of Shakespeare in the early 1590s were so intent on telling the saga of emergent nationhood, they exhibit a strong tendency to identify villains and heroes. Shakespeare is writing dramas, not schoolbook texts, and he freely alters dates and facts and emphases. Lord Talbot in *Henry VI, Part 1* is a hero because he dies defending English interests against the corrupt French. In *Henry VI, Part 2* Humphrey, duke of Gloucester, is cut down by opportunists because he represents the best interests of the commoners and the nation as a whole. Most of all, Richard of Gloucester is made out to be a villain epitomizing the very worst features of a chaotic century of civil strife. He foments strife, lies, and murders and makes outrageous promises he has no intention of keeping. He is a brilliantly theatrical figure because he is so inventive and clever, but he is also deeply threatening. Shakespeare gives him every defect that popular tradition imagined: a hunchback, a baleful glittering eye, a conspiratorial genius. The real Richard was no such villain, it seems. At least, his politically inspired murders were no worse than the systematic elimination of all opposition by his successor, the historical Henry VII. The difference is that Henry VII lived to commission historians to tell the story his way, whereas Richard lost everything through defeat. As founder of the Tudor dynasty and grandfather of Queen Elizabeth, Henry VII could command a respect that even Shakespeare was bound to honour, and accordingly the Henry Tudor that he portrays at the end of *Richard III* is a God-fearing patriot and loving husband of the Yorkist princess who is to give birth to the next generation of Tudor monarchs.

Richard III is a tremendous play, both in length and in the bravura depiction of its titular protagonist. It is called a tragedy on its original title page, as are other of these early English history plays. Certainly they present us with brutal deaths and with instructive falls of great men from positions of high authority to degradation and misery. Yet these plays are not tragedies in the Classical sense of the term. They contain so much else, and notably they end on a major key: the accession to power of the Tudor dynasty that will give England its great years under Elizabeth. The story line is one of suffering and of eventual salvation, of

deliverance by mighty forces of history and of divine over-
sight that will not allow England to continue to suffer
once she has returned to the true path of duty and decency.
In this important sense, the early history plays are like
tragicomedies or romances.

Plays of the Middle and Late Years

All Shakespeare's comedies share a belief in the positive,
health-giving powers of play. None, however, is completely
innocent of doubts about the limits that encroach upon
the comic space. Yet the confusions and contradictions of
Shakespeare's age find their highest expression in his tragedies. In these extraordinary achievements, all values,
hierarchies, and forms are tested and found wanting, and
all society's latent conflicts are activated.

Romantic Comedies

In the second half of the 1590s, Shakespeare brought to
perfection the genre of romantic comedy that he had
helped to invent. *A Midsummer Night's Dream* (c. 1595–96),
one of the most successful of all his plays, displays the kind
of multiple plotting he had practiced in *The Taming of the
Shrew* and other earlier comedies. The overarching plot is
of Duke Theseus of Athens and his impending marriage to
an Amazonian warrior, Hippolyta, whom Theseus has
recently conquered and brought back to Athens to be his
bride. Their marriage ends the play. They share this concluding ceremony with the four young lovers--Hermia and
Lysander, Helena and Demetrius--who have fled into the
forest nearby to escape the Athenian law and to pursue
one another, whereupon they are subjected to a complicated series of mix-ups. Eventually all is righted by fairy
magic, though the fairies are no less at strife. Oberon, king

of the fairies, quarrels with his Queen Titania over a changeling boy and punishes her by causing her to fall in love with an Athenian artisan who wears an ass's head. The artisans are in the forest to rehearse a play for the forthcoming marriage of Theseus and Hippolyta. Thus four separate strands or plots interact with one another. Despite the play's brevity, it is a masterpiece of artful construction.

The use of multiple plots encourages a varied treatment of the experiencing of love. For the two young human couples, falling in love is quite hazardous. The long-standing friendship between the two young women is threatened and almost destroyed by the rivalries of heterosexual encounter. The eventual transition to heterosexual marriage seems to them to have been a process of dreaming, indeed of nightmare, from which they emerge miraculously restored to their best selves. Meantime the marital strife of Oberon and Titania is, more disturbingly, one in which the female is humiliated until she submits to the will of her husband. Similarly, Hippolyta is an Amazon warrior queen who has had to submit to the authority of a husband. Fathers and daughters are no less at strife until, as in a dream, all is resolved by the magic of Puck and Oberon. Love is ambivalently both an enduring ideal relationship and a struggle for mastery in which the male has the upper hand.

The Merchant of Venice (c. 1596–97) uses a double plot structure to contrast a tale of romantic wooing with one that comes close to tragedy. Portia is a fine example of a romantic heroine in Shakespeare's mature comedies: she is witty, rich, exacting in what she expects of men, and adept at putting herself in a male disguise to make her presence felt. She is loyally obedient to her father's will and yet determined that she shall have Bassanio. She triumphantly resolves the murky legal affairs of Venice when the men have all failed. Shylock, the Jewish moneylender, is at the point of exacting a pound of flesh from Bassanio's friend Antonio as payment for a forfeited loan. Portia foils him in his attempt in a way that is both clever and shystering. Sympathy is uneasily balanced in Shakespeare's portrayal of Shylock, who is both persecuted by his Christian opponents and all too ready to demand an eye for an eye according to ancient law. Ultimately Portia triumphs, not only with Shylock in the court of law but in her marriage with Bassanio.

Much Ado About Nothing (c. 1598–99) revisits the issue of power struggles in courtship, again in a revealingly double plot. The young heroine of the more conventional story, derived from Italianate fiction, is wooed by a respectable young aristocrat named Claudio who has won his spurs and now considers it his pleasant duty to take a wife. He knows so little about Hero (as she is named) that he gullibly credits the contrived evidence of the play's villain, Don John, that she has had many lovers, including one on the evening before the intended wedding. Other men as well, including Claudio's senior officer, Don Pedro, and Hero's father, Leonato, are all too ready to believe the slanderous accusation. Only comic circumstances rescue Hero from her accusers and reveal to the men that they have been fools. Meantime, Hero's cousin, Beatrice, finds it hard to overcome her skepticism about men, even when she is wooed by Benedick, who is also a skeptic about marriage. Here the barriers to romantic understanding are inner and psychological and must be defeated by the good-natured plotting of their friends, who see that Beatrice and Benedick are truly made for one another in their wit and candour if they can only overcome their fear of being outwitted by each other. In what could be regarded as a brilliant rewriting of *The Taming of the Shrew*, the witty battle of the sexes is no less amusing and complicated, but the eventual accommodation finds something much closer to mutual respect and equality between men and women.

Rosalind, in *As You Like It* (c. 1598–1600), makes use of the by-now familiar device of disguise as a young man in order to pursue the ends of promoting a rich and substantial relationship between the sexes. As in other of these plays, Rosalind is more emotionally stable and mature than her young man, Orlando. He lacks formal education and is all rough edges, though fundamentally decent and attractive. She is the daughter of the banished Duke who finds herself obliged, in turn, to go into banishment with her dear cousin Celia and the court fool, Touchstone. Although Rosalind's male disguise is at first a means of survival in a seemingly inhospitable forest, it soon serves a more interesting function. As "Ganymede," Rosalind befriends Orlando, offering him counseling in the affairs of love. Orlando, much in need of such advice, readily accepts and proceeds to woo his "Rosalind" ("Ganymede" playing her own self) as though she were indeed a woman. Her wryly amusing perspectives on the follies of young love helpfully puncture Orlando's inflated and unrealistic "Petrarchan" stance as the young lover who writes poems to his mistress and sticks them up on trees. Once he has learned that love is not a fantasy of invented attitudes, Orlando is ready to be the husband of the real young woman (actually a boy actor, of course) who is presented to him as the transformed Ganymede-Rosalind. Other figures in the play further an understanding of love's glorious foolishness by their various attitudes: Silvius, the pale-faced wooer out of pastoral romance; Phoebe, the disdainful mistress whom he worships; William, the country bumpkin, and Audrey, the country wench; and, surveying and commenting on every imaginable kind of human folly, the clown Touchstone and the malcontent traveler Jaques.

The program cover from a 1901 production of Twelfth Night. *The play uses the dramatic convention of a woman disguised as a man, which is a recurring theme in Shakespeare's comedies.* Hulton Archive/Getty Images

Twelfth Night (c. 1600–02) pursues a similar motif of female disguise. Viola, cast ashore in Illyria by a shipwreck and obliged to disguise herself as a young man in order to gain a place in the court of Duke Orsino, falls in love with the duke and uses her disguise as a cover for an educational process not unlike that given by Rosalind to Orlando. Orsino is as unrealistic a lover as one could hope to imagine. He pays fruitless court to the Countess Olivia and seems content with the unproductive love melancholy in which he wallows. Only Viola, as "Cesario," is able to awaken in him a genuine feeling for friendship and love. They become inseparable companions and then seeming rivals for the hand of Olivia until the presto change of Shakespeare's stage magic is able to restore "Cesario" to her woman's garments and thus present to Orsino the flesh-and-blood woman whom he has only distantly imagined. The transition from same-sex friendship to heterosexual union is a constant in Shakespearean comedy. The woman is the self-knowing, constant, loyal one. The man needs to learn a lot from the woman. As in the other plays as well, *Twelfth Night* neatly plays off this courtship theme with a second plot, of Malvolio's self-deception that he is desired by Olivia—an illusion that can be addressed only by the satirical devices of exposure and humiliation.

The Merry Wives of Windsor (c. 1597–1601) is an interesting deviation from the usual Shakespearean romantic comedy in that it is set not in some imagined far-off place like Illyria or Belmont or the forest of Athens but in Windsor, a solidly bourgeois village near Windsor Castle in the heart of England. Uncertain tradition has it that Queen Elizabeth wanted to see Falstaff in love. There is little, however, in the way of romantic wooing (the story of Anne Page and her suitor Fenton is rather buried in the midst of so many other goings-on), but the play's portrayal of women, and especially of the two "merry wives," Mistress Alice Ford and Mistress Margaret Page, reaffirms what is so often true of women in these early plays, that they are good-hearted, chastely loyal, and wittily self-possessed. Falstaff, a suitable butt for their cleverness, is a scapegoat figure who must be publicly humiliated as a way of transferring onto him the human frailties that Windsor society wishes to expunge.

COMPLETION OF THE HISTORIES

Concurrent with his writing of these fine romantic comedies, Shakespeare also brought to completion (for the time being, at least) his project of writing 15th-century English history. After having finished in 1589–94 the tetralogy about Henry VI, Edward IV, and Richard III, bringing the story down to 1485, and then circa 1594–96 a play about John that deals with a chronological period (the 13th century) that sets it quite apart from his other history plays, Shakespeare turned to the late 14th and early 15th centuries and to the chronicle of Richard II, Henry IV, and Henry's legendary son Henry V. This inversion of historical order in the two tetralogies allowed Shakespeare to finish his sweep of late medieval English history with Henry V, a hero king in a way that Richard III could never pretend to be.

Richard II (c. 1595–96), written throughout in blank verse, is a sombre play about political impasse. It contains almost no humour, other than a wry scene in which the new king, Henry IV, must adjudicate the competing claims of the Duke of York and his Duchess, the first of whom wishes to see his son Aumerle executed for treason and the second of whom begs for mercy. Henry is able to be merciful on this occasion, since he has now won the kingship, and thus gives to this scene an upbeat movement. Earlier, however, the mood is grim. Richard, installed at an early age into the kingship, proves irresponsible as a ruler. He unfairly banishes his own first cousin, Henry Bolingbroke (later to be Henry IV), whereas the king himself appears to be guilty of ordering the murder of an uncle. When Richard keeps the dukedom of Lancaster from Bolingbroke without proper legal authority, he manages to alienate many nobles and to encourage Bolingbroke's return from exile. That return, too, is illegal, but it is a fact, and, when several of the nobles (including York) come over to Bolingbroke's side, Richard is forced to abdicate. The rights and wrongs of this power struggle are masterfully ambiguous. History proceeds without any sense of moral imperative. Henry IV is a more capable ruler, but his authority is tarnished by his crimes (including his seeming assent to the execution of Richard), and his own rebellion appears to teach the barons to rebel against him in turn. Henry eventually dies a disappointed man.

The dying king Henry IV must turn royal authority over to young Hal, or Henry, now Henry V. The prospect is dismal both to the dying king and to the members of his court, for Prince Hal has distinguished himself to this point mainly by his penchant for keeping company with the disreputable if engaging Falstaff. The son's attempts at reconciliation with the father succeed temporarily, especially when Hal saves his father's life at the battle of Shrewsbury, but (especially in *Henry IV, Part 2*) his reputation as wastrel will not leave him. Everyone expects from him a reign of irresponsible license, with Falstaff in an influential position. It is for these reasons that the young king must publicly repudiate his old companion of the tavern and the highway, however much that repudiation tugs at his heart and the audience's. Falstaff, for all his debauchery and irresponsibility, is infectiously amusing and delightful. He represents in Hal a spirit of youthful vitality that is left behind only with the greatest of regret as the young man assumes manhood and the role of crown prince. Hal manages all this with aplomb and goes on to defeat the French mightily at the Battle of Agincourt. Even his high jinks are a part of what is so attractive in him. Maturity and position come at a great personal cost: Hal becomes less a frail human being and more the figure of royal authority.

Thus, in his plays of the 1590s, the young Shakespeare concentrated to a remarkable extent on romantic comedies and English history plays. The two genres are nicely complementary: the one deals with courtship and marriage, while the other examines the career of a young man growing up to be a worthy king. Only at the end of the history plays does Henry V have any kind of romantic relationship with a woman, and this one instance is quite unlike courtships in the romantic comedies: Hal is given the Princess of France as his prize, his reward for sturdy manhood. He takes the lead in the wooing scene in which he invites her to join him in a political marriage. In both romantic comedies and English history plays, a young man successfully negotiates the hazardous and potentially rewarding paths of sexual and social maturation.

ROMEO AND JULIET

Apart from the early *Titus Andronicus*, the only other play that Shakespeare wrote prior to 1599 that is classified as a tragedy is *Romeo and Juliet* (*c*. 1594–96), which is quite untypical of the tragedies that were to follow. Written more or less at the time when Shakespeare was writing *A Midsummer Night's Dream*, *Romeo and Juliet* shares many of the characteristics of romantic comedy. Romeo and Juliet are not persons of extraordinary social rank or position, like Hamlet, Othello, King Lear, and Macbeth. They are the boy and girl next door, interesting not for their philosophical ideas but for their appealing love for each other. They are character types more suited to Classical comedy in that they do not derive from the upper class. Their wealthy families are essentially bourgeois. The eagerness with which Capulet and his wife court Count Paris as their prospective son-in-law bespeaks their desire for social advancement.

Accordingly, the first half of *Romeo and Juliet* is very funny, while its delight in verse forms reminds us of *A Midsummer Night's Dream*. The bawdry of Mercutio and of the Nurse is richly suited to the comic texture of the opening scenes. Romeo, haplessly in love with a Rosaline whom we never meet, is a partly comic figure like Silvius in *As You Like It*. The plucky and self-knowing Juliet is much like the heroines of romantic comedies. She is able to instruct Romeo in the ways of speaking candidly and unaffectedly about their love rather than in the frayed cadences of the Petrarchan wooer.

The battle scene from Romeo and Juliet, *between the Montagues and Capulets, marks the play's passage from pseudo-romantic comedy to outright tragedy.* Kean Collection/Hulton Archive/Getty Images

The play is ultimately a tragedy, of course, and indeed warns its audience at the start that the lovers are "star-crossed." Yet the tragic vision is not remotely that of *Hamlet* or *King Lear*. Romeo and Juliet are unremarkable, nice young people doomed by a host of considerations outside themselves: the enmity of their two families, the misunderstandings that prevent Juliet from being able to tell her parents whom it is that she has married, and even unfortunate coincidence (such as the misdirection of the letter sent to Romeo to warn him of the Friar's plan for Juliet's recovery from a deathlike sleep). Yet there is the element of personal responsibility upon which most mature tragedy rests when Romeo chooses to avenge the death of Mercutio by killing Tybalt, knowing that this deed will undo the soft graces of forbearance that Juliet has taught him. Romeo succumbs to the macho peer pressure of his male companions, and tragedy results in part from this choice. Yet so much is at work that the reader ultimately sees *Romeo and Juliet* as a love tragedy—celebrating the exquisite brevity of young love, regretting an unfeeling world, and evoking an emotional response that differs from that produced by the other tragedies. Romeo and Juliet are, at last, "Poor sacrifices of our enmity" (Act V, scene 3, line 304). The emotional response the play evokes is a strong one, but it is not like the response called forth by the tragedies after 1599.

THE "PROBLEM" PLAYS

Whatever his reasons, about 1599–1600 Shakespeare turned with unsparing intensity to the exploration of darker issues such as revenge, sexual jealousy, aging, midlife crisis, and death. Perhaps he saw that his own life was moving into a new phase of more complex and vexing experiences. Perhaps he felt, or sensed, that he had worked through the romantic comedy and history play and the emotional trajectories of maturation that they encompassed. At any event, he began writing not only his great tragedies but a group of plays that are hard to classify in terms of genre. They are sometimes grouped today as "problem" plays or "problem" comedies. An examination of these plays is crucial to understanding this period of transition from 1599 to 1605.

The three problem plays dating from these years are *All's Well That Ends Well*, *Measure for Measure*, and *Troilus and Cressida*. *All's Well* is a comedy ending in acceptance of marriage but in a way that poses thorny ethical issues. Count Bertram cannot initially accept his marriage to Helena, a woman of lower social station who has grown up in his noble household and has won Bertram as her husband by her seemingly miraculous cure of the French king. Bertram's reluctance to face the responsibilities of marriage is all the more dismaying when he turns his amorous intentions to a Florentine maiden, Diana, whom he wishes to seduce without marriage. Helena's stratagem to resolve this difficulty is the so-called bed trick, substituting herself in Bertram's bed for the arranged assignation and then calling her wayward husband to account when she is pregnant with his child. Her ends are achieved by such morally ambiguous means that marriage seems at best a precarious institution on which to base the presumed reassurances of romantic comedy. The pathway toward resolution and emotional maturity is not easy. Helena is a more ambiguous heroine than Rosalind or Viola.

Measure for Measure (c. 1603–04) similarly employs the bed trick, and for a similar purpose, though in even murkier circumstances. Isabella, on the verge of becoming a nun, learns that she has attracted the sexual desire of Lord Angelo, the deputy ruler of Vienna serving in the mysterious absence of the Duke. Her plea to Angelo for her brother's life, when that brother (Claudio) has been sentenced to die for fornication with his fiancée, is met with a demand that she sleep with Angelo or forfeit Claudio's life. This ethical dilemma is resolved by a trick (devised by the Duke, in disguise) to substitute for Isabella a woman (Mariana) whom Angelo was supposed to marry but refused when she could produce no dowry. The Duke's motivations in manipulating these substitutions and false appearances are unclear, though arguably his wish is to see what the various characters of this play will do when faced with seemingly impossible choices. Angelo is revealed as a morally fallen man, a would-be seducer and murderer who is nonetheless remorseful and ultimately glad to have been prevented from carrying out his intended crimes. Claudio learns that he is coward enough to wish to live by any means, including the emotional and physical blackmail of his sister. And Isabella learns that she is capable of bitterness and hatred, even if, crucially, she finally discovers that she can and must forgive her enemy. Her charity, and the Duke's stratagems, make possible an ending in forgiveness and marriage, but in that process the nature and meaning of marriage are severely tested.

Troilus and Cressida (c. 1601–02) is the most experimental and puzzling of these three plays. Simply in terms of genre, it is virtually unclassifiable. It can hardly be a comedy, ending as it does in the deaths of Patroclus and Hector and the looming defeat of the Trojans. Nor is the ending normative in terms of romantic comedy: the lovers, Troilus and Cressida, are separated from one another and embittered by the failure of their relationship. The play is a history play in a sense, dealing as it does with the great Trojan War celebrated in Homer's *Iliad*, and yet its purpose is hardly that of telling the story of the war. As a tragedy, it is perplexing in that the chief figures of the play (apart from Hector) do not die at the end, and the mood is one of desolation and even disgust rather than tragic catharsis. Perhaps the play should be thought of as a satire. The choric observations of Thersites and Pandarus serve throughout as a mordant commentary on the interconnectedness of war and lechery. With fitting ambiguity, the play was placed in the Folio of 1623 between the histories and the tragedies, in a category all by itself. Clearly, in these problem plays Shakespeare was opening up for himself a host of new problems in terms of genre and human sexuality.

JULIUS CAESAR

Written in 1599 (the same year as *Henry V*) or 1600, probably for the opening of the Globe Theatre on the south bank of the Thames, *Julius Caesar* illustrates similarly the transition in Shakespeare's writing toward darker themes and tragedy. It, too, is a history play in a sense, dealing with a non-Christian civilization existing 16 centuries before Shakespeare wrote his plays. Roman history opened up for Shakespeare a world in which divine purpose could not be easily ascertained. The characters of *Julius Caesar* variously interpret the great event of the assassination of Caesar as one in which the gods are angry or disinterested or capricious or simply not there. The wise Cicero observes, "Men may construe things after their fashion, / Clean from the purpose of the things themselves" (Act I, scene 3, lines 34–35).

Human history in *Julius Caesar* seems to follow a pattern of rise and fall, in a way that is cyclical rather than divinely purposeful. Caesar enjoys his days of triumph until he is cut down by the conspirators. Brutus and Cassius succeed to power but not for long. Brutus's attempts to protect Roman republicanism and the freedom of the city's citizens to govern themselves through senatorial tradition end up in the destruction of the very liberties he most cherished. He and Cassius meet their destiny at the Battle of Philippi. They are truly tragic figures, especially Brutus, in that their essential characters are their fate. Brutus is a good man but also proud and stubborn, and these latter qualities ultimately bring about his death. Shakespeare's first major tragedy is Roman in spirit and Classical in its notion of tragic character. It shows what Shakespeare had to learn from Classical precedent as he set about looking for workable models in tragedy.

THE TRAGEDIES

Hamlet (c. 1599–1601), on the other hand, chooses a tragic model closer to that of *Titus Andronicus* and Kyd's The *Spanish Tragedy*. In form, *Hamlet* is a revenge tragedy. It features characteristics found in Titus as well: a protagonist charged with the responsibility of avenging a heinous crime against the protagonist's family, a cunning antagonist, the appearance of the ghost of the murdered person, the feigning of madness to throw off the villain's suspicions, the play within the play as a means of testing the villain, and still more.

Yet to search out these comparisons is to highlight what is so extraordinary about *Hamlet*, for it refuses to be merely a revenge tragedy. Shakespeare's protagonist is unique in the genre in his moral qualms, and most of all in his finding a way to carry out his dread command without becoming a cold-blooded murderer. Hamlet does act bloodily, especially when he kills Polonius, thinking that the old man hidden in Gertrude's chambers must be the King whom Hamlet is commissioned to kill. The act seems plausible and strongly motivated, and yet Hamlet sees at once that he has erred. He has killed the wrong man, even if Polonius has brought this on himself with his incessant spying. Hamlet sees that he has offended heaven and that he will have to pay for his act. When, at the play's end, Hamlet encounters his fate in a duel with Polonius's son, Laertes, Hamlet interprets his own tragic story as one that Providence has made meaningful. By placing himself in the hands of Providence and believing devoutly that "There's a divinity that shapes our ends, / Rough-hew them how we will" (Act V, scene 2, lines 10–11), Hamlet finds himself ready for a death that he has longed for. He also finds an opportunity for killing Claudius almost unpremeditatedly, spontaneously, as an act of reprisal for all that Claudius has done.

Hamlet thus finds tragic meaning in his own story. More broadly, too, he has searched for meaning in dilemmas of all sorts: his mother's overhasty marriage, Ophelia's weak-willed succumbing to the will of her father and brother, his being spied on by his erstwhile friends Rosencrantz and Guildenstern, and much more. His utterances are often despondent, relentlessly honest, and philosophically profound, as he ponders the nature of friendship, memory, romantic attachment, filial love, sensuous enslavement, corrupting habits (drinking, sexual lust), and almost every phase of human experience.

One remarkable aspect about Shakespeare's great tragedies (*Hamlet*, *Othello*, *King Lear*, *Macbeth*, and *Antony and Cleopatra* most of all) is that they proceed through such a staggering range of human emotions, and especially the emotions that are appropriate to the mature years of the human cycle. Hamlet is 30, one learns—an age when a person is apt to perceive that the world around him is "an unweeded garden / That grows to seed. Things rank and gross in nature / Possess it merely" (Act I, scene 2, lines 135–137). Shakespeare was about 36 when he wrote this play. *Othello* (c. 1603–04) centres on sexual jealousy in marriage. *King Lear* (c. 1605–06) is about aging, generational conflict, and feelings of ingratitude. Macbeth (c. 1606–07) explores ambition mad enough to kill a father figure who stands in the way. *Antony and Cleopatra*, written about 1606–07 when Shakespeare was 42 or thereabouts, studies the exhilarating but ultimately dismaying phenomenon of midlife crisis. Shakespeare moves his readers vicariously through these life experiences while he himself struggles to capture, in tragic form, their terrors and challenges.

These plays are deeply concerned with domestic and family relationships. In *Othello* Desdemona is the only daughter of Brabantio, an aging senator of Venice, who dies heartbroken because his daughter has eloped with a dark-skinned man who is her senior by many years and is of another culture. With Othello, Desdemona is briefly happy, despite her filial disobedience, until a terrible sexual jealousy is awakened in him, quite without cause other than his own fears and susceptibility to Iago's insinuations that it is only "natural" for Desdemona to seek erotic pleasure with a young man who shares her background. Driven by his own deeply irrational fear and hatred of women and seemingly mistrustful of his own masculinity, Iago can assuage his own inner torment only by persuading other men like Othello that their inevitable fate is to be cuckolded. As a tragedy, the play adroitly exemplifies the traditional Classical model of a good man brought to misfortune by hamartia, or tragic flaw. As Othello grieves, he is one who has "loved not wisely, but too well" (Act V, scene 2, line 354). It bears remembering, however, that Shakespeare owed no loyalty to this Classical model. *Hamlet*, for one, is a play that does not work well in Aristotelian terms. The search for an Aristotelian hamartia has led all too often to the trite argument that Hamlet suffers from melancholia and a tragic inability to act, whereas a more plausible reading of the play argues that finding the right course of action is highly problematic for him and for everyone. Hamlet sees examples on all sides of those whose forthright actions lead to fatal mistakes or absurd ironies (Laertes, Fortinbras), and indeed his own swift killing of the man he assumes to be Claudius hidden in his mother's chambers turns out to be a mistake for which he realizes heaven will hold him accountable.

Daughters and fathers are also at the heart of the major dilemma in *King Lear*. In this configuration, Shakespeare does what he often does in his late plays: erase the wife from the picture, so that father and daughter(s) are left to deal with one another. (Compare *Othello*, *The Winter's Tale*, *Cymbeline*, *The Tempest*, and perhaps the circumstances of Shakespeare's own life, in which his relations with his daughter Susanna especially seem to have meant more to him than his partly estranged marriage with Anne.) Lear's banishing of his favourite daughter, Cordelia, because of her laconic refusal to proclaim a love for him as the essence of her being, brings upon this aging king the terrible punishment of being belittled and rejected by his ungrateful daughters, Goneril and Regan. Concurrently, in the play's second plot, the Earl of Gloucester makes a similar mistake with his good-hearted son, Edgar, and thereby delivers himself into the hands of his scheming bastard son, Edmund. Both these erring elderly fathers are ultimately nurtured by the loyal children they have banished, but not before the play has tested to its absolute limit the proposition that evil can flourish in a bad world.

The gods seem indifferent, perhaps absent entirely. Pleas to them for assistance go unheeded while the storm of fortune rains down on the heads of those who have trusted in conventional pieties. Part of what is so great in this play is that its testing of the major characters requires them to seek out philosophical answers that can arm the resolute heart against ingratitude and misfortune by constantly pointing out that life owes one nothing. The consolations of philosophy preciously found out by Edgar and Cordelia are those that rely not on the suppositious gods but on an inner moral strength demanding that one be charitable and honest because life is otherwise monstrous and subhuman. The play exacts terrible prices of those who persevere in goodness, but it leaves them and the reader, or audience, with the reassurance that it is simply better to be a Cordelia than to be a Goneril, to be an Edgar than to be an Edmund.

Macbeth is in some ways Shakespeare's most unsettling tragedy, because it invites the intense examination of the heart of a man who is well-intentioned in most ways but who discovers that he cannot resist the temptation to achieve power at any cost. Macbeth is a sensitive, even poetic person, and as such he understands with frightening clarity the stakes that are involved in his contemplated deed of murder. Duncan is a virtuous king and

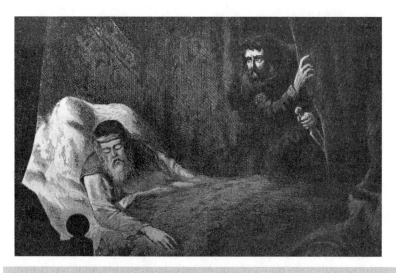

Artist Robert Dudley's depiction of Duncan's murder from Shakespeare's Macbeth. *One of the playwright's shorter works,* Macbeth *does not include the subplots found in many of Shakespeare's other plays.* Hulton Archive/ Getty Images

his guest. The deed is regicide and murder and a violation of the sacred obligations of hospitality. Macbeth knows that Duncan's virtues, like angels, "trumpet-tongued," will plead against "the deep damnation of his taking-off" (Act I, scene 7, lines 19–20). The only factor weighing on the other side is personal ambition, which Macbeth understands to be a moral failing. The question of why he proceeds to murder is partly answered by the insidious temptations of the three Weird Sisters, who sense Macbeth's vulnerability to their prophecies, and the terrifying strength of his wife, who drives him on to the murder by describing his reluctance as unmanliness. Ultimately, though, the responsibility lies with Macbeth. His collapse of moral integrity confronts the audience and perhaps implicates it. The loyalty and decency of such characters as Macduff hardly offset what is so painfully weak in the play's protagonist.

Antony and Cleopatra approaches human frailty in terms that are less spiritually terrifying. The story of the lovers is certainly one of worldly failure. Plutarch's *Lives* gave to Shakespeare the object lesson of a brave general who lost his reputation and sense of self-worth through his infatuation with an admittedly attractive but nonetheless dangerous woman. Shakespeare changes none of the circumstances: Antony hates himself for dallying in Egypt with Cleopatra, agrees to marry with Octavius Caesar's sister Octavia as a way of recovering his status in the Roman triumvirate, cheats on Octavia eventually, loses the battle of Actium because of his fatal attraction for Cleopatra, and dies in Egypt a defeated, aging warrior. Shakespeare adds to this narrative a compelling portrait of midlife crisis. Antony is deeply anxious about his loss of sexual potency and position in the world of affairs. His amorous life in Egypt is manifestly an attempt to affirm and recover his dwindling male power.

Yet the Roman model is not in Shakespeare's play the unassailably virtuous choice that it is in Plutarch. In *Antony and Cleopatra* Roman behaviour does promote attentiveness to duty and worldly achievement, but, as embodied in young Octavius, it is also obsessively male and cynical about women. Octavius is intent on capturing Cleopatra and leading her in triumph back to Rome—that is, to cage the unruly woman and place her under male control. When Cleopatra perceives that aim, she chooses a noble suicide rather than humiliation by a patriarchal male. In her suicide, Cleopatra avers that she has called "great Caesar ass / Unpolicied" (Act V, scene 2, lines 307–308). Vastly to be preferred is the fleeting dream of greatness with Antony, both of them unfettered, godlike, like Isis and Osiris, immortalized as heroic lovers even if the actual circumstances of their lives were often disappointing and even tawdry. The vision in this tragedy is deliberately unstable, but at its most ethereal it encourages a vision of human greatness that is distant from the soul-corrupting evil of *Macbeth* or *King Lear*.

Two late tragedies also choose the ancient Classical world as their setting but do so in a deeply dispiriting way. Shakespeare appears to have been much preoccupied with ingratitude and human greed in these years. *Timon of Athens* (c. 1605–08), probably an unfinished play and possibly never produced, initially shows us a prosperous man fabled for his generosity. When he discovers that he has exceeded his means, he turns to his seeming friends for the kinds of assistance he has given them, only to discover that their memories are short. Retiring to a bitter isolation, Timon rails against all humanity and refuses every sort of consolation, even that of well-meant companionship and sympathy from a former servant. He dies in isolation. The unrelieved bitterness of this account is only partly ameliorated by the story of the military captain Alcibiades, who has also been the subject of Athenian ingratitude and forgetfulness but who manages to reassert his authority at the end. Alcibiades resolves to make some accommodation with the wretched condition of humanity. Timon will have none of it. Seldom has a more unrelievedly embittered play been written.

Coriolanus (*c.* 1608) similarly portrays the ungrateful responses of a city toward its military hero. The problem is complicated by the fact that Coriolanus, egged on by his mother and his conservative allies, undertakes a political role in Rome for which he is not temperamentally fitted. His friends urge him to hold off his intemperate speech until he is voted into office, but Coriolanus is too plain-spoken to be tactful in this way. His contempt for the plebeians and their political leaders, the tribunes, is unsparing. His political philosophy, while relentlessly aristocratic and snobbish, is consistent and theoretically sophisticated. The citizens are, as he argues, incapable of governing themselves judiciously. Yet his fury only makes matters worse and leads to an exile from which he returns to conquer his own city, in league with his old enemy and friend, Aufidius. When his mother comes out for the city to plead for her life and that of other Romans, he relents and thereupon falls into defeat as a kind of mother's boy, unable to assert his own sense of self. As a tragedy, *Coriolanus* is again bitter, satirical, ending in defeat and humiliation. It is an immensely powerful play, and it captures a philosophical mood of nihilism and bitterness that hovers over Shakespeare's writings throughout these years in the first decade of the 1600s.

THE ROMANCES

Concurrently, nonetheless, and then in the years that followed, Shakespeare turned again to the writing of comedy. The late comedies are usually called romances or tragicomedies because they tell stories of wandering and separation leading eventually to tearful and joyous reunion. They are suffused with a bittersweet mood that seems eloquently appropriate to a writer who has explored with such unsparing honesty the depths of human suffering and degradation in the great tragedies.

Pericles, written perhaps in 1606–08 and based on the familiar tale of Apollonius of Tyre, may involve some collaboration of authorship. The text is unusually imperfect, and it did not appear in the Folio of 1623. It employs a chorus figure, John Gower (author of an earlier version of this story), to guide the reader or viewer around the Mediterranean on Pericles's various travels, as he avoids marriage with the daughter of the incestuous King Antiochus of Antioch; marries Thaisa, the daughter of King Simonides of Pentapolis; has a child by her; believes his wife to have died in childbirth during a storm at sea and has her body thrown overboard to quiet the superstitious fears of the sailors; puts his daughter, Marina, in the care of Cleon of Tarsus and his wicked wife, Dionyza; and is eventually restored to his wife and child after many years. The story is typical romance. Shakespeare adds touching scenes of reunion and a perception that beneath the naive account of travel lies a subtle dramatization of separation, loss, and recovery. Pericles is deeply burdened by his loss and perhaps, too, a sense of guilt for having consented to consign his wife's body to the sea. He is recovered from his despair only by the ministrations of a loving daughter, who is able to give him a reason to live again and then to be reunited with his wife.

The Winter's Tale (*c.* 1609–11) is in some ways a replaying of this same story, in that King Leontes of Sicilia, smitten by an irrational jealousy of his wife, Hermione, brings about the seeming death of that wife and the real death of their son. The resulting guilt is unbearable for Leontes

and yet ultimately curative over a period of many years
that are required for his only daughter, Perdita (whom he
has nearly killed also), to grow to maturity in distant
Bohemia. This story, too, is based on a prose romance, in
this case Robert Greene's *Pandosto*. The reunion with
daughter and then wife is deeply touching as in *Pericles*,
with the added magical touch that the audience does not
know that Hermione is alive and in fact has been told that
she is dead. Her wonderfully staged appearance as a statue
coming to life is one of the great theatrical coups in
Shakespeare, playing as it does with favourite
Shakespearean themes in these late plays of the minister-
ing daughter, the guilt-ridden husband, and the
miraculously recovered wife. The story is all the more
moving when one considers that Shakespeare may have
had, or imagined, a similar experience of attempting to
recover a relationship with his wife, Anne, whom he had
left in Stratford during his many years in London.

In *Cymbeline* (c. 1608–10) King Cymbeline drives his
virtuous daughter Imogen into exile by his opposition to
her marriage with Posthumus Leonatus. The wife in this
case is Cymbeline's baleful Queen, a stereotypical wicked
stepmother whose witless and lecherous son Cloten
(Imogen's half brother) is the embodiment of everything
that threatens and postpones the eventual happy ending
of this tale. Posthumus, too, fails Imogen by being irratio-
nally jealous of her, but he is eventually recovered to a
belief in her goodness. The dark portraiture of the Queen
illustrates how ambivalent is Shakespeare's view of the
mother in his late plays. This Queen is the wicked stepmother, like Dionyza in *Pericles*. In her relentless desire for
control, she also brings to mind Lady Macbeth and the
Weird Sisters in *Macbeth*, as well as Coriolanus's mother,
Volumnia. The devouring mother is a forbidding presence
in the late plays, though she is counterbalanced by

redeeming maternal figures such as Hermione in *The Winter's Tale* and Thaisa in *Pericles*.

The Tempest (c. 1611) sums up much of what Shakespeare's mature art was all about. Once again we find a wifeless father with a daughter, in this case on a deserted island where the father, Prospero, is entirely responsible for his daughter's education. He behaves like a dramatist in charge of the whole play as well, arranging her life and that of the other characters. He employs a storm at sea to bring young Ferdinand into the company of his daughter. Ferdinand is Prospero's choice, because such a marriage will resolve the bitter dispute between Milan and Naples—arising after the latter supported Prospero's usurping brother Antonio in his claim to the dukedom of Milan—that has led to Prospero's banishment. At the same time, Ferdinand is certainly Miranda's choice as well. The two fall instantly in love, anticipating the desired romantic happy ending. The ending will also mean an end to Prospero's career as artist and dramatist, for he is nearing retirement and senses that his gift will not stay with him forever. The imprisoned spirit Ariel, embodiment of that temporary and precious gift, must be freed in the play's closing moments. Caliban, too, must be freed, since Prospero has done what he could to educate and civilize this Natural Man. Art can only go so far.

The Tempest seems to have been intended as Shakespeare's farewell to the theatre. It contains moving passages of reflection on what his powers as artist have been able to accomplish, and valedictory themes of closure. As a comedy, it demonstrates perfectly the way that Shakespeare was able to combine precise artistic construction (the play chooses on this farewell occasion to observe the Classical unities of time, place, and action) with his special flair for stories that transcend the merely human and physical: *The Tempest* is peopled with spirits,

One of Shakespeare's last plays, The Tempest *offers a mix of comedy and drama, classical dramatic construction, and the fantastic.* Kean Collection/ Hulton Archive/Getty Images

monsters, and drolleries. This, it seems, is Shakespeare's summation of his art as comic dramatist.

But *The Tempest* proved not to be Shakespeare's last play after all. Perhaps he discovered, as many people do, that he was bored in retirement in 1613 or thereabouts. No doubt his acting company was eager to have him back. He wrote a history play titled *Henry VIII* (1613), which is extraordinary in a number of ways: it relates historical events substantially later chronologically than those of the 15th century that had been his subject in his earlier historical plays. It is separated from the last of those plays by perhaps 14 years. And, perhaps most significant, it is as much romance as history play. History in this instance is really about the birth of Elizabeth I, who was to become England's great queen. The circumstances of Henry VIII's troubled marital affairs, his meeting with Anne Boleyn, his confrontation with the papacy, and all the rest turn out to be the humanly unpredictable ways by which Providence engineers the miracle of Elizabeth's birth. The play ends with this great event and sees in it a justification and necessity of all that has proeceded. Thus history yields its providential meaning in the shape of a play that is both history and romance.

The Poems

Shakespeare seems to have wanted to be a poet as much as he sought to succeed in the theatre. His plays are wonderfully and poetically written, often in blank verse. And when he experienced a pause in his theatrical career about 1592–94, the plague having closed down much theatrical activity, he wrote poems. *Venus and Adonis* (1593) and *The Rape of Lucrece* (1594) are the only works that Shakespeare seems to have shepherded through the printing process. Both owe a good deal to Ovid, the Classical poet whose writings Shakespeare encountered repeatedly in school. These two poems are the only works for which he wrote dedicatory prefaces; both are to Henry Wriothesley, earl of Southampton. This young man, a favourite at court, seems to have encouraged Shakespeare and to have served for a brief time at least as his sponsor. The dedication to the second poem is measurably warmer than the first. An unreliable tradition supposes that Southampton gave Shakespeare the stake he needed to buy into the newly formed Lord Chamberlain's acting company in 1594. Shakespeare became an actor-sharer, one of the owners in a capitalist enterprise that shared the risks and the gains among them. This company succeeded brilliantly. Shakespeare and his colleagues, including Richard Burbage, John Heminge, Henry Condell, and Will Sly, became wealthy through their dramatic presentations.

Shakespeare may also have written at least some of his sonnets to Southampton, beginning in these same years of 1593–94 and continuing on through the decade and later. The question of autobiographical basis in the sonnets is much debated, but Southampton at least fits the portrait of a young gentleman who is being urged to marry and produce a family. (Southampton's family was eager that he do just this.) Whether the account of a strong, loving relationship between the poet and his gentleman friend is autobiographical is more difficult still to determine. As a narrative, the sonnet sequence tells of strong attachment, of jealousy, of grief at separation, of joy at being together and sharing beautiful experiences. The emphasis on the importance of poetry as a way of eternizing human achievement and of creating a lasting memory for the poet himself is appropriate to a friendship between a poet of modest social station and a friend who is better-born. When the sonnet sequence introduces the so-called "Dark Lady," the narrative becomes one of painful and

SHAKE-SPEARES

SONNETS.

Neuer before Imprinted.

AT LONDON
By G. Eld for T. T. and are
to be folde by Iohn Wright, dwelling
at Chriſt Church gate.
1609.

The title page the first published version of Shakespeare's sonnets. They had circulated in manuscript prior to 1609. Hulton Archive/Getty Images

destructive jealousy. Scholars do not know the order in which the sonnets were composed—Shakespeare seems to have had no part in publishing them—but no order other than the order of publication has been proposed, and, as the sonnets stand, they tell a coherent and disturbing tale. The poet experiences sex as something that fills him with revulsion and remorse, at least in the lustful circumstances in which he encounters it. His attachment to the young man is a love relationship that sustains him at times more than the love of the Dark Lady can do, and yet this loving friendship also dooms the poet to disappointment and self-hatred. Whether the sequence reflects any circumstances in Shakespeare's personal life, it certainly is told with an immediacy and dramatic power that bespeak an extraordinary gift for seeing into the human heart and its sorrows.

Collaborations and Spurious Attributions

The Two Noble Kinsmen (*c*. 1612–14) brought Shakespeare into collaboration with John Fletcher, his successor as chief playwright for the King's Men. (Fletcher is sometimes thought also to have helped Shakespeare with *Henry VIII*.) The story, taken out of Chaucer's "Knight's Tale," is essentially another romance, in which two young gallants compete for the hand of Emilia and in which deities preside over the choice. Shakespeare may have had a hand earlier as well in *Edward III*, a history play of about 1590–95, and he seems to have provided a scene or so for *The Book of Sir Thomas More* (*c*. 1593–1601) when that play encountered trouble with the censor.

Collaborative writing was common in the Renaissance English stage, and it is not surprising that Shakespeare was called upon to do some of it. Nor is it surprising that, given his towering reputation, he was credited with having written a number of plays that he had nothing to do with, including those that were spuriously added to the third edition of the Folio in 1664: *Locrine* (1591–95), *Sir John Oldcastle* (1599–1600), *Thomas Lord Cromwell* (1599–1602), *The London Prodigal* (1603–05), *The Puritan* (1606), and *A Yorkshire Tragedy* (1605–08). To a remarkable extent, nonetheless, his corpus stands as a coherent body of his own work. The shape of his career has a symmetry and internal beauty not unlike that of the individual plays and poems.

QUESTIONS OF AUTHORSHIP

Readers and playgoers in Shakespeare's own lifetime, and indeed until the late 18th century, never questioned Shakespeare's authorship of his plays. He was a well-known actor from Stratford who performed in London's premier acting company, among the great actors of his day. He was widely known by the leading writers of his time as well, including Ben Jonson and John Webster, both of whom praised him as a dramatist. Many other tributes to him as a great writer appeared during his lifetime. Any theory that supposes him not to have been the writer of the plays and poems attributed to him must suppose that Shakespeare's contemporaries were universally fooled by some kind of secret arrangement.

Yet suspicions on the subject gained increasing force in the mid-19th century. One Delia Bacon proposed that the author was her claimed ancestor Sir Francis Bacon, Viscount St. Albans, who was indeed a prominent writer of the Elizabethan era. What had prompted this theory? The chief considerations seem to have been that little is known about Shakespeare's life (though in fact more is known about him than about his contemporary writers), that he was from the country town of Stratford-upon-Avon, that he never attended one of the universities, and that therefore it would have been impossible for him to write knowledgeably about the great affairs of English courtly life such as we find in the plays.

The theory is suspect on a number of counts. University training in Shakespeare's day centred on theology and on Latin, Greek, and Hebrew texts of a sort that would not have greatly improved Shakespeare's knowledge of contemporary English life. By the 19th century, a university education was becoming more and more the mark of a broadly educated person, but university training in the

16th century was quite a different matter. The notion that only a university-educated person could write of life at court and among the gentry is an erroneous and indeed a snobbish assumption. Shakespeare was better off going to London as he did, seeing and writing plays, listening to how people talked. He was a reporter, in effect. The great writers of his era (or indeed of most eras) are not usually aristocrats, who have no need to earn a living by their pens. Shakespeare's social background is essentially like that of his best contemporaries. Edmund Spenser went to Cambridge, it is true, but he came from a sail-making family. Christopher Marlowe also attended Cambridge, but his kindred were shoemakers in Canterbury. John Webster, Thomas Dekker, and Thomas Middleton came from similar backgrounds. They discovered that they were writers, able to make a living off their talent, and they (excluding the poet Spenser) flocked to the London theatres where customers for their wares were to be found. Like them, Shakespeare was a man of the commercial theatre.

Other candidates—William Stanley, 6th earl of Derby, and Christopher Marlowe among them—have been proposed, and indeed the very fact of so many candidates makes one suspicious of the claims of any one person. The late 20th-century candidate for the writing of Shakespeare's plays, other than Shakespeare himself, was Edward de Vere, 17th earl of Oxford. Oxford did indeed write verse, as did other gentlemen. Sonneteering was a mark of gentlemanly distinction. Oxford was also a wretched man who abused his wife and drove his father-in-law to distraction. Most seriously damaging to Oxford's candidacy is the fact that he died in 1604. The chronology presented here, summarizing perhaps 200 years of assiduous scholarship, establishes a professional career for Shakespeare as dramatist that extends from about 1589 to 1614. Many of his greatest plays—*King Lear*, *Antony and Cleopatra*, and *The Tempest*, to name but three—were written after 1604. To suppose that the dating of the canon is totally out of whack and that all the plays and poems were written before 1604 is a desperate argument. Some individual dates are uncertain, but the overall pattern is coherent. The growth in poetic and dramatic styles, the development of themes and subjects, along with objective evidence, all support a chronology that extends to about 1614. To suppose alternatively that Oxford wrote the plays and poems before 1604 and then put them away in a drawer, to be brought out after his death and updated to make them appear timely, is to invent an answer to a nonexistent problem.

When all is said, the sensible question one must ask is, why would Oxford want to write the plays and poems and then not claim them for himself? The answer given is that he was an aristocrat and that writing for the theatre was not elegant. Hence he needed a front man, an alias. Shakespeare, the actor, was a suitable choice. But is it plausible that a cover-up like this could have succeeded?

Shakespeare's contemporaries, after all, wrote of him unequivocally as the author of the plays. Ben Jonson, who knew him well, contributed verses to the First Folio of 1623, where (as elsewhere) he criticizes and praises Shakespeare as the author. John Heminge and Henry Condell, fellow actors and theatre owners with Shakespeare, signed the dedication and a foreword to the First Folio and described their methods as editors. In his own day, therefore, he was accepted as the author of the plays. In an age that loved gossip and mystery as much as any, it seems hardly conceivable that Jonson and Shakespeare's theatrical associates shared the secret of a gigantic literary hoax without a single leak or that they

To the Reader.

This Figure, that thou here feeft put,
    It was for gentle Shakefpeare cut;
Wherein the Graver had a ftrife
    VVith Nature, to out-doo the life :
O, could he but have drawne his VVit
    As well in Braffe, as he hath hit
His Face; the Print vvould then furpaffe
    All, that vvas ever vvrit in Braffe.
But, fince he cannot, Reader, looke
    Not on his Picture, but his Booke.

B. I.

Ben Jonson's dedication in the First Folio of Shakespeare's collected plays.
Hulton Archive/Getty Images

could have been imposed upon without suspicion. Unsupported assertions that the author of the plays was a man of great learning and that Shakespeare of Stratford was an illiterate rustic no longer carry weight, and only when a believer in Bacon or Oxford or Marlowe produces sound evidence will scholars pay close attention.

PLAYWRIGHTS AFTER SHAKESPEARE

Shakespeare's perception of a crisis in public norms and private belief became the overriding concern of the drama until the closing of the theatres in 1642. The prevailing manner of the playwrights who succeeded him was realistic, satirical, and antiromantic, and their plays focused predominantly on those two symbolic locations, the city and the court, with their typical activities, the pursuit of wealth and power. "Riches and glory," wrote Sir Walter Raleigh, "Machiavel's two marks to shoot at," had become the universal aims, and this situation was addressed by city comedies and tragedies of state. Increasingly, it was on the stages that the rethinking of early Stuart assumptions took place.

On the one hand, in the works of Thomas Heywood, Thomas Dekker, John Day, Samuel Rowley, and others, the old tradition of festive comedy was reoriented toward the celebration of confidence in the dynamically expanding commercial metropolis. Heywood claimed to have been involved in some 200 plays, and they include fantastic adventures starring citizen heroes, spirited, patriotic, and inclined to a leveling attitude in social matters. His masterpiece, *A Woman Killed with Kindness* (1603), is a middle-class tragedy. Dekker was a kindred spirit, best seen in his *Shoemakers' Holiday* (1599), a celebration of citizen brotherliness and Dick Whittington-like success. The play nevertheless faces squarely up to the hardships of work, thrift, and the contempt of the great. On the other hand, the very industriousness that the likes of Heywood viewed with civic pride became in the hands of Ben Jonson, George Chapman, John Marston, and Thomas Middleton a sign of self-seeking, avarice, and anarchy, symptomatic of the sicknesses in society at large.

BEN JONSON

The crucial innovations in satiric comedy were made by Ben Jonson, Shakespeare's friend and nearest rival, who stands at the fountainhead of what subsequently became

The plays of Ben Jonson set the tone for subsequent comedic theatre. The use of satire without condemnation is a hallmark of Jonson's oeuvre. Hulton Archive/Getty Images

the dominant modern comic tradition. His early plays, particularly *Every Man in His Humour* (1598) and *Every Man Out of His Humour* (1599), with their galleries of grotesques, scornful detachment, and rather academic effect, were patently indebted to the verse satires of the 1590s. They introduced to the English stage a vigorous and direct anatomizing of "the time's deformities," the language, habits, and humours of the London scene.

Jonson began as a self-appointed social legislator, socially conservative but intellectually radical, outraged by a society given over to inordinate appetite and egotism, and ambitious through his mammoth learning to establish himself as the privileged artist, the fearless and faithful mentor and companion to kings. But he was ill at ease with a court inclined in its masques to prefer flattery to judicious advice. Consequently the greater satires that followed are marked by their gradual accommodations with popular comedy and by their unwillingness to make their implied moral judgments explicit: in *Volpone* (1606) the theatrical brilliance of the villain easily eclipses the sordid legacy hunters whom he deceives; *Epicoene* (1609) is a noisy farce of metropolitan fashion and frivolity; *The Alchemist* (1610) exhibits the conjurings and deceptions of clever London rogues; and *Bartholomew Fair* (1614) draws a rich portrait of city life parading through the annual fair at Smithfield, a vast panorama of a society given over to folly. In these plays, fools and rogues are indulged to the very height of their daring, forcing upon the audience both criticism and admiration. The strategy leaves the audience to draw its own conclusions while liberating Jonson's wealth of exuberant comic invention, virtuoso skill with plot construction, and mastery of a language tumbling with detailed observation of London's multifarious ephemera.

After 1616 Jonson abandoned the stage for the court, but, finding himself increasingly disregarded, he made a hard-won return to the theatres. The most notable of his late plays are popular in style: *The New Inn* (1629), which has affinities with the Shakespearean romance, and *A Tale of a Tub* (1633), which resurrects the Elizabethan country farce.

OTHER JACOBEAN DRAMATISTS

Of Jonson's successors in city comedy, Francis Beaumont, in *The Knight of the Burning Pestle* (1607), amusingly insults the citizenry while ridiculing its taste for romantic plays. John Marston adopts so sharp a satirical tone that his comic plays frequently border on tragedy. All values are mocked by Marston's bitter and universal skepticism. His city comedy *The Dutch Courtezan* (1605), set in London, explores the pleasures and perils of libertinism. His tragicomedy *The Malcontent* (1604) is remarkable for its wild language and sexual and political disgust. Marston cuts the audience adrift from the moorings of reason by a dizzying interplay of parody and seriousness.

Only in the city comedies of Thomas Middleton was Jonson's moral concern with greed and self-ignorance bypassed, for Middleton presents the pursuit of money as the sole human absolute and buying and selling, usury, law, and the wooing of rich widows as the dominant modes of social interaction. His unprejudiced satire touches the actions of citizen and gentleman with equal irony and detachment. The only operative distinction is between fool and knave, and the sympathies of the audience are typically engaged on the side of wit, with the resourceful prodigal and dexterous whore. His characteristic form, used in *Michaelmas Term* (1605) and *A Trick to Catch the Old One* (1606), was intrigue comedy, which enabled him to portray his society dynamically, as a mechanism in which each sex and class pursues its own selfish interests. He was thus concerned less with characterizing individuals in depth than with examining the inequalities and injustices of the world that cause them to behave as they do. His *The Roaring Girl* (c. 1608) and *A Chaste Maid in Cheapside* (1613) are the only Jacobean comedies to rival the comprehensiveness of *Bartholomew Fair*, but their social attitudes are opposed to Jonson's. The misbehaviour that Jonson condemned morally as "humours" or affectation Middleton understands as the product of circumstance.

Middleton's social concerns are also powerfully to the fore in his great tragedies, *Women Beware Women* (c. 1621) and *The Changeling* (1622), in which the moral complacency of men of rank is shattered by the dreadful violence they themselves have casually set in train, proving the answerability of all men for their actions despite the exemptions claimed for privilege and status. The hand of heaven is even more explicitly at work in the overthrow of the aristocratic libertine D'Amville in Cyril Tourneur's *The Atheist's Tragedy* (c. 1611), where the breakdown of old codes of deference before a progressive middle-class morality is strongly in evidence. In *The Revenger's Tragedy* (1607), now generally attributed to Middleton, a scathing attack on courtly dissipation is reinforced by complaints about inflation and penury in the countryside at large.

For more traditionally minded playwrights, new anxieties lay in the corrupt and sprawling bureaucracy of the modern court and in the political eclipse of the nobility before incipient royal absolutism. In Jonson's *Sejanus* (1603) Machiavellian statesmen abound, while George Chapman's *Bussy d'Ambois* (1604) and *Conspiracy of Charles, Duke of Byron* (1608) drew on recent French history to chart the collision of the magnificent but redundant heroism of the old-style aristocrat, whose code of honour had outlived its social function, with pragmatic arbitrary monarchy. Chapman doubtless had the career and fate of Essex in mind. The classic tragedies of state are John Webster's, with their dark Italian courts, intrigue and treachery, spies, malcontents, and informers. His *The White Devil* (1612), a divided, ambivalent play, elicits sympathy even for a vicious heroine, since she is at the mercy of her deeply corrupt society, and the heroine in *The Duchess of Malfi* (1623) is the one decent and spirited inhabitant of her world, yet her noble death cannot avert the fearfully futile and haphazard carnage that ensues. As so often on the Jacobean stage, the challenge to the male-dominated world of power was mounted through the experience of its women.

THE LAST RENAISSANCE DRAMATISTS

Already in the Jacobean period, signs of a politer drama such as would prevail after 1660 were beginning to appear. Simply in terms of productivity and longevity, the most successful Jacobean playwright was John Fletcher, whose ingenious tragicomedies and sometimes bawdy comedies were calculated to attract the applause of the emerging Stuart leisured classes. With plays such as *The Faithful Shepherdess* (1609 or 1610), Fletcher caught up with the latest in avant-garde Italianate drama, while his most dazzling comedy, *The Wild Goose Chase* (produced 1621, printed 1652), is a battle of the sexes set among Parisian gallants and their ladies. It anticipates the Restoration comedy of manners. Fletcher's successor in the reign of Charles I was James Shirley, who showed even greater facility with romantic comedy and the mirroring of fashions and foibles. In *The Lady of Pleasure* (1635) and *Hyde Park* (1637), Shirley presented the fashionable world to itself in its favourite haunts and situations.

Prolific Jacobean dramatist John Fletcher wrote clever tragicomedies as well as lewd comedies specifically to garner acclaim from the emerging leisure classes. He frequently collaborated with Francis Beaumont. Hulton Archive/ Getty Images

However, the underlying tensions of the time continued to preoccupy the drama of the other major Caroline playwrights: John Ford, Philip Massinger, and Richard Brome. The plays of Ford, the last major tragic dramatist of the Renaissance, focus on profoundly conservative societies whose values are in crisis. In 'Tis Pity She's a Whore (1633?), a seemingly typical middle-class family is destroyed by the discovery of incest. In The Broken Heart (1633?), a courtly society collapses under the pressure of hidden political maladies. Massinger, too, wrote some fine tragedies (The Roman Actor, 1626), but his best plays are comedies and tragicomedies preoccupied with political themes, such as The Bondman (1623), which deals with issues of liberty and obedience, and A New Way to Pay Old Debts (performed 1625, printed 1633), which satirizes the behaviour and outlook of the provincial gentry. The tradition of subversive domestic satire was carried down to the English Civil Wars in the plays of Brome, whose anarchic and popular comedies, such as The Antipodes (1640) and A Jovial Crew (produced 1641, printed 1652), poke fun at all levels of society and include caustic and occasionally libelous humour. The outbreak of fighting in 1642 forced the playhouses to close, but this was not because the theatre had become identified with the court. Rather, a theatre of complex political sympathies was still being produced. The crisis in which the playhouses had become embroiled had been the drama's preoccupation for three generations.

The maturation of English literature from the Old English period through the Renaissance is nothing short of remarkable. Within this span lies a substantial body of work that represents the culture and times, yet breaks free from those constraints as well. Certain authors and compositions stood out, yet even lesser-known footnotes from this period laid the groundwork for the striking strides in style, language, content, and overall sophistication of the written word. Most important, during this period was the introduction of the printing press to the British Isles, a revolutionary development whose effects still reverberate today.

One of the many transformations in literary works was that authors moved from recounting relatively simple existing tales and biblical stories to creating deeply thoughtful, and thought-provoking, prose, poetry, and drama. A multitude of societal tensions and upheavals during this period drove authors to create in an attempt to make sense of the world around them and wrest meaning out of their very existence. The result was a highly personal record of the times, conveyed in dramatic and narrative form. By creating this record, they also were presaging the work of all later writers. In this sense, Caedmon is an equal to—perhaps even a contemporary of—James Joyce. Despite living 1,300 years apart, they both used their work to find meaning amidst upheaval. Another result was an array of compelling stories—from the likes of Chaucer, Donne, Malory, Milton, and the greatest of all playwrights, William Shakespeare—that continue to enthrall readers to this day. English literature had changed greatly between the 7th and 17th centuries. But there was still much more to come.

acrostic A short verse composition, so constructed that the initial letters of the lines, taken consecutively, form words.

allegory A symbolic fictional narrative that conveys a meaning not explicitly set forth in the narrative.

amanuensis One employed to write from dictation or to copy a manuscript.

aphoristic Having to do with a concise statement of a principle or an adage.

assonance A relatively close repetition of sounds, especially of vowels, or a repetition of vowels without repetition of consonants that is used as an alternative to rhyme in verse.

bourgeois Having to do with the middle class or with a person influenced by private-property interest.

bravura A show of daring or brilliance.

eclogues Short pastoral poems on the subject of rural life in which, typically, shepherds converse.

ennui A feeling of weariness, dissatisfaction, or boredom.

episcopacy A government of the church by bishops or by a hierarchy.

euphuism An Elizabethan literary style marked by excessive use of balance, antithesis, and alliteration and by frequent use of similes drawn from mythology and nature.

fabliau A short, usually comic, frankly coarse, and often cynical tale in verse popular in the 12th and 13th centuries.

hermetic Impervious to external influence.

humanism The revival of classical letters, individualistic critical spirit, and emphasis on secular concerns characteristic of the Renaissance.

Metaphysical Having to do with poetry of the 17th century that is highly intellectual and philiosophical and marked by unconventional imagery.

obliquity Deviation from moral rectitude or sound thinking.

panegyrics Eulogistic orations or writings; formal or elaborate praises.

pastoral A poem or play dealing with shepherds or rural life in an often artificial manner and typically drawing a contrast between the innocence and serenity of a simple rural life and the corruption of city or courtly life.

polemicists Those who attack or refute the opinions or principles of another.

prolusions Academic exercises of the 17th century used by students to apply their learning in logic and rhetoric that were presented in the manner of a debate.

quiddities Trifling points.

sophistry Subtly deceptive reasoning.

stultifying Causing to appear to be illogical, foolish, or absurd.

supernal Being of or coming from on high; heavenly.

vicissitudes Natural changes or mutations that can be seen in nature or human affairs; the difficulties attendant with a particular way of life, career, or course of action.

THE OLD ENGLISH PERIOD

R.D. Fulk and Christopher M. Cain, *A History of Old English Literature* (2002), is an excellent introductory survey of both the literature and critical trends. Derek Pearsall, *Old English and Middle English Poetry* (1977), is a good critical survey of both periods. Elaine Treharne (ed.), *Old and Middle English: An Anthology*, 2nd ed. (2004), presents an extensive selection of works; the more-difficult texts are accompanied by translations. S.A.J. Bradley (trans. and ed.), *Anglo-Saxon Poetry* (1982, reissued 1995), anthologizes prose translations of Old English poems.

THE MIDDLE ENGLISH PERIOD

Two good general approaches are A.S.G. Edwards (ed.), *Middle English Prose: A Critical Guide to Major Authors and Genres* (1984), which includes bibliographies and surveys of scholarship; and David Wallace (ed.), *The Cambridge History of Medieval English Literature* (1999), on literature after the Norman Conquest. R.M. Wilson, *Early Middle English Literature*, 3rd ed. (1968), critically surveys this period. J.A.W. Bennett and G.V. Smithers (eds.), *Early Middle English Verse and Prose*, 2nd ed. (1968, reissued 1982), is an authoritative anthology, with a glossary. J.B. Trapp, Douglas Gray, and Julia Boffey (eds.), *Medieval English Literature*, 2nd ed. (2002), is another useful anthology.

Analytic studies include David Aers, *Community, Gender, and Individual Identity: English Writing, 1360–1430* (1988); Piero Boitani, *English Medieval Narrative in the Thirteenth and Fourteenth Centuries* (1982; originally published in Italian, 1980); Nancy Mason Bradbury, *Writing Aloud: Storytelling in Late Medieval England* (1998); J.A. Burrow, *The Ages of Man: A Study in Medieval Writing and Thought* (1986); Ruth Evans and Lesley Johnson (eds.), *Feminist Readings in Middle English Literature* (1994); David Lawton (ed.), *Middle English Alliterative Poetry and Its Literary Background* (1982); C.S. Lewis, *The Allegory of Love: A Study in Medieval Tradition* (1936, reissued 1995); Robert Potter, *The English Morality Play* (1975); and A.C. Spearing, *Medieval to Renaissance in English Poetry* (1985).

THE RENAISSANCE PERIOD, 1550–1660

ELIZABETHAN POETRY AND PROSE

In terms of material covered, C.S. Lewis, *English Literature in the Sixteenth Century, Excluding the Drama* (1954, reprinted 1997), remains without rival, although some of its judgments now seem very dated. Also impressive for its coverage is David Loewenstein and Janel Mueller (eds.), *The Cambridge History of Early Modern English Literature* (2002), which has essays on topics surveying the whole field. A less-ambitious collection, though still highly useful, is Michael Hattaway (ed.), *A Companion to English Renaissance Literature and Culture* (2000). Challenging and provocative reinterpretations of the period are Stephen Greenblatt, *Renaissance Self-Fashioning* (1980, reissued 2005); and David Norbrook, *Poetry and*

Politics in the English Renaissance, rev. ed. (2002). Works devoted to particular topics include Gary Waller, *English Poetry of the Sixteenth Century*, 2nd ed. (1993); J.W. Lever, *The Elizabethan Love Sonnet*, 2nd ed. (1966, reprinted 1978); and Linda Woodbridge, *Women and the English Renaissance* (1984).

EARLY STUART POETRY AND PROSE

The most-detailed general narrative (though dated) is Douglas Bush, *English Literature in the Earlier Seventeenth Century, 1600–1660*, 2nd ed., rev. (1962, reissued 1979). More useful are Thomas N. Corns, *The Cambridge Companion to English Poetry: Donne to Marvell* (1993); Alan Sinfield, *Literature in Protestant England, 1560–1660* (1983); and Alison Shell, *Catholicism, Controversy, and the English Literary Imagination, 1558–1660* (1999). Among studies on prose is Roger Pooley, *English Prose of the Seventeenth Century* (1992). Nigel Smith, *Literature and Revolution in England, 1640–1660* (1994), discusses the Civil War period.

ELIZABETHAN AND EARLY STUART DRAMA

The most authoritative late-20th-century overview is G.K. Hunter, *English Drama 1586–1642* (1997). Surveys that are more user-friendly are presented in vol. 3 and 4 of Clifford Leech and T.W. Craik (eds.), *The Revels History of Drama in English*, 8 vol. (1976–83, reprinted 1996), which cover 1576 to 1613 and 1613 to 1660, respectively. Alexander Leggatt, *English Drama: Shakespeare to the Restoration, 1590–1660* (1988), is a reliable overview. Collections of helpful essays covering the entire period include A.R. Braunmuller and Michael Hattaway (eds.), *The Cambridge Companion to English Renaissance Drama,*

2nd ed. (2003); Arthur F. Kinney (ed.), *A Companion to Renaissance Drama* (2002); and Jane Milling and Peter Thomson (eds.), *The Cambridge History of British Theatre, Vol. 1: Origins to 1660* (2004). Among the studies of the politics of Renaissance drama are Margot Heinemann, *Puritanism and Theatre* (1980); and Jonathan Dollimore, *Radical Tragedy*, 3rd ed. (2004). Feminist studies include Lisa Jardine, *Still Harping on Daughters: Women and Drama in the Age of Shakespeare* (1983); and Kathleen McLuskie, *Renaissance Dramatists* (1989). Martin White, *Renaissance Drama in Action* (1998), discusses the stagecraft and conditions of playwriting.

INDEX